Copyright @ 2009
by Lisa Sandlin

Photographs @ 2008
Lisa Sandlin,

All rights reserved. No part of this book may be used or reproduced in any manner without the written permission of the Publisher.

Library of Congress Control Number: 9781439222102

ISBN: 1-4392-2210-X
Printed by Booksurge Publishing

Booksurge Publishing
7290-B Investment Dr
N. Charleston, SC 29418

Book Design by Jennifer Langan

Printed in the United States of America

To purchase additional copies of this book, please contact Booksurge Publishing at www.booksurge.com or visit www.amazon.com

Live Well,
Live Long,
Be Home!
Lisa Sandlin

Houses That Work
For Life!

A GUIDE TO CREATING HOMES THAT PROVIDE SECURITY, COMFORT AND EMPOWERMENT FOR ALL GENERATIONS.

ACKNOWLEDGEMENTS

I find it interesting to read acknowledgements and share the appreciation an author has for those that have inspired, supported and advised their work. It is now time for me to share my own.

First, I must acknowledge my grandmother and father. Both have passed on, but I feel assured that somehow they have been with me through the process of writing this book. Grandma was the inspiration for redirecting my life. Her pain and struggles sparked the awareness and inquiry of our housing standards. I thank my father for sharing his knowledge, wisdom and support throughout the years of my education and practice. In his final days, his affirmation of the importance of my work meant so much.

I cannot begin to express all the gratitude and admiration I have for Jennifer Langan, the graphic designer of this book. Jen is an extremely talented and dedicated design student at the University of Cincinnati. When I decided to move forward with this project, I knew she was the one I could depend on to help me pull it off. Her patience, support, dedication and immeasurable hours of work through this process, while attending classes, are remarkable. I deeply appreciate everything she has done and will forever be grateful.

Anyone who knows me understands the respect and idolization I have for my brother, Dale Murray. Dale is a professor of design at the University of Cincinnati and is the kindest, most brilliant and wittiest person I know. He guided, advised and criticized my work in the most tactful ways. He was always supportive and encouraging, but honest when constructive criticism was appropriate. I am extremely grateful to have him in my life, as a brother and as my mentor.

I want to thank Teresa Abrams, a friend and English teacher, for her guidance in editing and content review of the text. Her expertise and skills are very much appreciated.

I would like to extend a special thank you to all of my clients and friends for the use of images of their homes to aid in the understanding of the text. I gathered photos over my many years of practice and referred to my library of images for this book.

Finally, I must thank my family, my husband Jim, my mother Betty, my children, JB, Brandon, Tina and Lisa and grandchildren, Kylee, Haley, Lindsay and Mazzy for their encouragement, patience and support. Many hours were consumed in the making of this book, time away from my precious family and spent in front of my computer. My husband has taken over all the household chores, my mother always has an encouraging word and my children and grandchildren have been patiently awaiting my return into their lives.

ACKNOWLEDGEMENTS

This book is the completion of a long **journey** and hopefully the beginning of a new one. It began with an **inquiry** into housing that led to a formal education and evolved into a **design practice** that represents a new way of thinking about how we dwell. My dream for the future is for all housing to incorporate this **inclusive** philosophy. Thank you to all who have participated in this journey and thank you to all that will embrace its message and
change the way we dwell.

ABOUT THE AUTHOR

lisa sandlin

Lisa Sandlin is a mother, wife, daughter, business woman, and professor of architecture and interior design. As a young mother of four, Lisa helped with the care of her aging grandmother. Grandma lived in a single floor house built by Lisa's father. As her grandmother grew older and her health began to fail the ability to dwell in her home became more and more difficult. The bathing facility was dangerous and even with the aid of additional equipment it became impossible for her to perform the daily tasks of personal hygiene. The kitchen's gas range was unsafe, the laundry facilities were in the basement, and even though it was a ranch style house there were several steps in and out, making it inaccessible for her wheelchair. Grandma was forced to leave the place she had known as home for decades. This was a devastating experience for the entire family. It also instigated Lisa's inquiry into how and why most houses do not address the issues that may arise as we age.

Lisa enrolled in The School of Design, Architecture, Art, & Planning at the University of Cincinnati with the goal of learning how to design better houses. She quickly realized that little, if any, consideration to single family residential design was inherent to most design school's pedagogy.

With determination, she excelled through the program of Interior Design, researching design topics that included: Universal Design Theory, retirement community and long term healthcare, sacred spaces, interdisciplinary, furniture, and finally for her senior thesis, to the dismay of her professors, she chose to design a single family residence. The project, entitled From Infancy to Elderly, There's No Place Like Home was a prototype residence that addressed the ideals of: security, familiarity, flexibility and comfort through a Universal Design philosophy. Universal design is an approach that is inclusive of all people regardless of mental or physical ability.

ABOUT THE AUTHOR

Upon completion of her undergraduate degree, a bachelor of science in design, she was awarded a fellowship to continue her education in the graduate program in Architecture. Her master's thesis again dealt with residential design. It was a case study entitled "Moving Experiences: An examination of moving from and connecting to the places where we reside."

Throughout her education she practiced residential design. Her business evolved as her education progressed. For many years Lisa has been teaching design at Miami University, Oxford, Ohio and the University of Cincinnati focusing on Universal Design and Sustainability in a variety of studio and lecture courses.

Lisa's design practice incorporates research, analysis, education and collaboration with her clients. Together they have created houses that work now and will continue working to meet their needs as life progresses. Lisa practices "ethical design" which combines the philosophy of inclusive or trans-generational design with eco-friendly and sustainable design. These homes are extremely energy efficient, functional and empowering while providing the comfort and beauty one would expect in a custom designed home.

GRANDMA'S HOUSE AND PLAN

TABLE OF CONTENTS

1. Introduction
2. There's No Place Like Home
3. Housing Basics
4. "Standards" for Typical People
5. The Site – Orientation, Topography and Context
6. Public and Private Living
7. Creating Houses That Work for Life!
    - The Entries
    - Transitional Zones
    - The Kitchen
    - Personal Care Areas
    - Laundry Facilities
    - Sleeping Quarters
    - Business/Computers Stations
    - Eating Areas
    - Care Free Living
    - Inside Out and Outside In Places
    - Storage Spaces
    - Easy Maintenance
8. Conclusion

TABLE OF CONTENTS

1
7
15
23
39
49
55

119

INTRODUCTION

I

One thing we can count on in life is change. From the moment of birth we begin our journey into this constant state.

INTRODUCTION

Awareness and acceptance of a problem is considered the first step of its solution. I am introducing a problem that many of us might not realize exists. Most of our houses do not work; they do not provide us with a secure, comfortable and empowering environment for the duration of our lives.

Diversity and equality are virtues our society claims to respect and admire. We aspire to desegregate, to include all races, socioeconomic classes, religions and people with disabilities. Our housing; however expresses the opposite. The majority segregates generations, splits socioeconomic levels and disregards the physically challenged. Communities of specific age groups and those of similar socioeconomic levels are evident throughout the country. Our elders are enclosed in gated communities, nursing, assisted living and retirement homes. Those with physical challenges struggle to blend in.

Our homes are designed for the "typical person", people of average size, shape and physical abilities. These standards of the housing industry have evolved over many years of complacency by both the providers and the consumers of houses. We have generally been a society of compromise. We settle in our homes and dwell in the manner that the house dictates.

Even with the marvels of modern medicine the aging process can have a profound effect on our bodies.

When needs change we may modify, but most just make do until the time comes that we are forced to move from our home.

One thing we can count on in life is change. From the moment of birth we begin our journey into this constant state. Our bodies and minds grow and develop; we experience infancy, childhood, adolescence, adulthood, and if we are fortunate, we live long enough to reach full maturity and gain the wisdom that being an elder brings. As children we face challenges because we are small, as we grow those challenges diminish but new ones may arise. Young adulthood poses even different needs especially when we become parents. When facing retirement or the empty nester phase, our requirements usually change once again. And when we are old, our bodies tire and tend to fail. Even with the marvels of modern medicine the aging process can have a profound effect on our bodies.

INTRODUCTION

When we are young adults and venturing into home ownership we give little thought to the challenges that life can bring. Unless you have been a caregiver or personally experienced a major surgery, illness or injury, you probably can't relate to the difficulties that can occur while living in a typical house. Try getting to a second floor bedroom after abdominal surgery or while on crutches. Maneuvering in a standard bathroom can be quite difficult even with the slightest disability.

Residential designers, developers, contractors, and home builders should realize that the majority of the houses they are building by the thousands across the country are poorly designed from a functional standpoint. From low cost housing to the most luxurious estates, most houses do not offer a well researched, developed, or flexible floor plan.

This book is a result of years of research and practice and compiles a set of guidelines to aid homeowners, designers and builders in the creation of houses that work for life. These design principles work for the design of new homes or may be applied to existing houses.

Houses that work for life has two meanings. First, these homes empower the residents and adapt to challenges that may occur through all stages of life. Secondly, in a broader sense, through sustainable practices, support and address the quality of life on the planet. This trans-generational or aging-in-place design philosophy coincides with sustainability by virtue of longevity of usefulness. Houses that work for life incorporate eco-friendly materials and energy efficiency. These homes strive to work in collaboration with nature. Houses that work for life, work for people and planet.

The idea for a better kind of house began when I experienced the situation with my grandmother and shared in the heartache she felt when forced to leave her home. My generation, the baby boomers, is now facing these same issues personally or with our own parents.

76 million Americans born between 1945 and 1964 represent the generation referred to as the "Baby Boomers" and are 39% of Americans over the age of 18.

INTRODUCTION

We are a demanding generation and are not willing to settle or compromise as easily as previous generations did. We are beginning to understand that the philosophy of creating houses that are empowering and flexible is a good idea. Many boomers are experiencing first hand that their homes, or their parent's homes, just don't work when physical or mental abilities change. This dose of reality has sparked an increased interest in the trans-generational or aging-in-place design practice.

Going "green" is another popular trend in society. The rise of energy costs and desire to consume less is generating the awareness of the positive results we can make within our own home. Either for economic or ethical reasons, energy efficiency is a good thing; you may believe in the theory of global warming or not, but a low energy bill at the end of the month is always welcomed.

Houses That Work For Life! is a book full of information, graphics, and images to guide you in the creation of homes that provide security, comfort, and empowerment for all generations.

We will:

- Explore the psychological aspects of home.
- Discuss housing basics and look at popular typical designs.
- Learn design principles that improve the experiential quality of life.
- Go through descriptive guidelines for each space of the home to create houses that work for life.

Housing is usually categorized within different price ranges and types. They range from the most modest to the most luxurious. Houses that work for life can come in all sizes, styles, and prices. They address accessibility issues, but the attributes don't end there. These houses are visit-able, flexible in usage, safe, energy efficient and provide everyone with all the comforts of home.

My goal for this book is to inspire and motivate all people, especially those in the housing industry to question the way we typically dwell. Whether remodeling, renovating or building new homes we must strive to create ethically designed homes that provide shelter for the body, security for the mind, and a sanctuary for the spirit.

INTRODUCTION

"We must strive to create ethically designed homes that provide shelter for the body, security for the mind, and a sanctuary for the spirit."

THERE'S NO PLACE LIKE HOME

2

As human beings we need shelter, but when a house is a home, it provides us with much, much more.

THERE'S NO PLACE LIKE HOME

A house that is comfortable, secure, personalized, familiar, and offers us sanctuary from the rest of the world is a home. It is a place to work, play, relax and feel inspired. The home is the core of the family, whatever type of family it might be. As human beings we need shelter, but when a house is a home, it provides us with much, much more.

A home is an expression of who we are. Spaces are personalized with color, art, and accessories. We bond with our homes and create a relationship with the spaces. Leaving our home can cause a feeling of discomfort. Even when on a luxurious vacation, most of us are comforted when we arrive back home. Many of us have experienced the feeling of being homesick. It can mean several different things; we may feel homesick for our native land, our family and friends, or the neighborhood, but sometimes we just miss the house.

A home provides places for our most cherished memories. Our memories are often attached to the places they occurred. Leaving a house where many memories were formed can be an extremely unsettling experience. It is a major step in our lives when we leave our childhood home to start a new life, we are excited and adventurous but we might discover some new emotions. As we near the end of our life's journey, leaving our home can be devastating. As we age, our memories become increasingly important to us and sometimes the physical presence of the place where memories occurred helps us remember.

Being forced to leave our home where it is no longer safe for us to reside is a common occurance. But even the security a new residence will provide, offers little comfort to those suffering from the feelings of being homesick.

These personal attachments and connections we have to the places we live are sometimes difficult to understand and overcome. It takes times to adjust and settle in to a new residence, time to personalize and bond with the new place and make it feel like home.

Moving from one house to another is considered one of life's most traumatic events.

THERE'S NO PLACE LIKE HOME

I had never experienced the trauma related to moving until my last move. I always had the opportunity to bond with the new home prior to moving into it. Either by building, remodeling, decorating, or just cleaning, the connection was made. This last time was different. We moved in quickly. My husband had made the decision to move immediately after we closed the deal. Papers were signed at five o'clock and we were in the house by nine. I was in grad school at the time and he thought it would be better for me if he took control and made the move. I didn't even have time to sweep the floor or wipe out the cabinets. He had solicited our family and friends to help and I was grateful, but I was not in control of the placement of my stuff in the new house. For days, I searched the kitchen for the items I needed and struggled to somehow bond with this new place. I felt like a stranger in someone else's house, I felt alienated in my own home. Finally, after months of cleaning, painting, and renovating the house became our home.

My grandmother never again felt the comfort and security a home provides after she was forced to leave her home of thirty years. She first resided with one of her sons but his house didn't work either. Much to her dismay and the dismay of her family she had to move into an assisted living facility where she shared a small room with a complete stranger until the time of her passing. The pleasure of being surrounded by personal things was limited to one chair, a dresser and a few accessories.

THERE'S NO PLACE LIKE HOME

We all should have the privilege of being comforted by the feelings a home provides at the end of our lives. My father recently passed away in his own home surrounded by his loved ones. After experiencing the trauma of my grandmother's move, staying at home was his dream.

Dad built their home years ago and it had never been remodeled, so many of the problems that often arise in typical houses were encountered. Dad could not stand for lengthy periods since a major surgery ten years prior. He needed to sit while showering so a shower chair had been installed over the tub in the master bath. The bathroom was too narrow to allow enough space for the wheelchair and passage for the hospice nurse to get around him and assist him onto the shower chair. He was too weak to accomplish this task on his own so showers ceased and he never again felt the pleasure of warm water flowing over his tired body. He tried to maintain the dignity of shaving himself, but couldn't use the sink unless awkwardly positioned. The bedroom was small, additional equipment was required for his care: a toilet chair at the side of the bed because the toilet in the bathroom was inaccessible, a hospital bed to ensure comfort and safety and a lounge chair for the nurse that never left the room. This resulted in very tight passageways for the many family members that frequented the room. The narrow door opening and hallway made it difficult to move the equipment and wheel chair in and out of the space, and at the end, when the funeral directors came, special provisions had to be made to remove him from his home. The challenges were great, compromises many, independence and dignity was lost, but with a lot of help, he was able to remain in his home.

THERE'S NO PLACE LIKE HOME

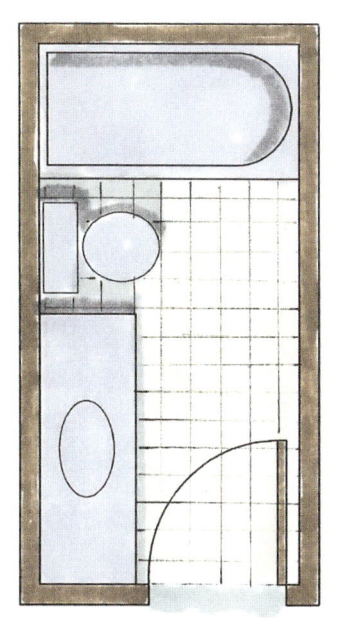

This is the same bathroom I attempted to care for my grandmother in, no revisions were ever made so my dad experienced the same difficulties.

For many years Dad and I shared stories and experiences of his home building business and my design practice. As he grew older and his physical abilities began to change he understood completely the importance of houses that work. With tears in his eyes as he struggled to use his bathroom, he looked at me and said "I get it". In the last week of his life, he told me once again how special my work is and how worthwhile and rewarding it must be. I have to say, I agree.

THERE'S NO PLACE LIKE HOME

Moving may be traumatic, but living through an extensive remodel or renovation can also cause a major disruption to your life. When our home is in shambles so is our life. Remodeling or extensively renovating a home can have the same psychological effects as moving into a different house; if a house is altered too much from its original state one might not feel that familiar sense of home. It is important for the residents to participate in the remodeling process so an attachment to the new environment is made.

If a person with disabilities continues to reside in the house during the renovation process, it is crucial that special procedures and provisions be implemented during the construction phase. Air quality, cleanliness, safety and accessibility must be maintained. Mentally disabled people might require additional considerations. Healthcare professionals can provide assistance with special need situations.

Human factors, ergonomics, and function play huge roles in commercial design applications but are rarely considered in residential design. If we put as much thought, research, and consideration into the design of our houses as we do for our work places and health care facilities the act of dwelling in our homes would surely improve. Our bathrooms would be safer and function better for everybody's size and physical ability, our kitchens would work for those of us that aren't standard height or don't have the ability to stand for lengthy periods of time. The space adjacencies would address current life styles, not those of years past. And in our golden years, those years when most of us are forced to leave our homes, we would be able to stay and age gracefully in the places we love and know as *home.*

I had the privilege of designing a new home for a husband and wife that intended to have both of their mothers reside with them. Together we created a great house that works really well for all of the occupants. Gary's mother passed away before its completion. Diana's mom resided in the home for six months before her passing. The day after her mother passed away, Diana called to thank me for designing such a beautiful home and making her mother's life so wonderful at the end.

THERE'S NO PLACE LIKE HOME

Similar to my grandmother's situation it was no longer possible for her mother to reside in her own home because of its inaccessibility and safety issues. While living in Diana's new house she was able to maintain some of her independence and dignity due to the aging-in-place philosophy implemented in the design. I was deeply touched by this phone call and am extremely grateful to have had the opportunity to make a difference in all their lives.

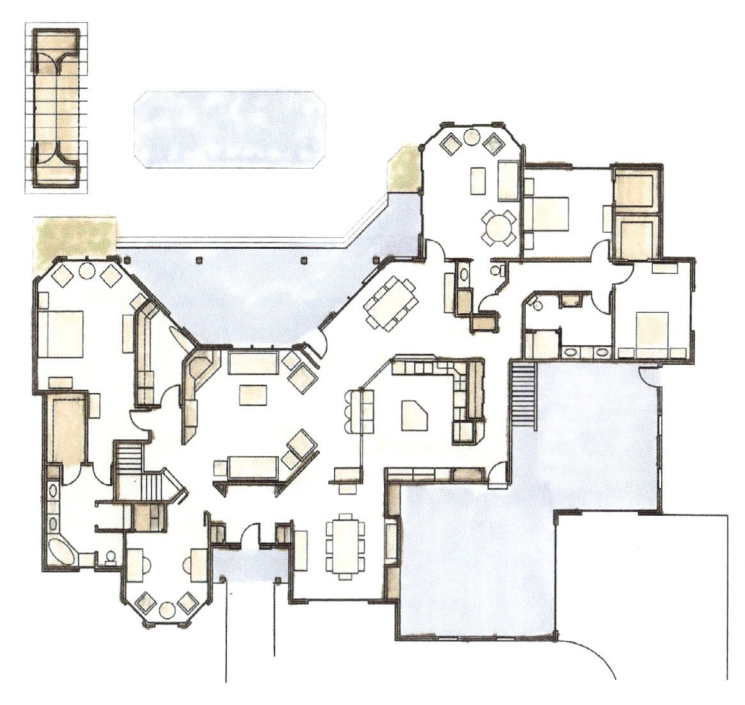

A second accessible bedroom and bathroom area enabled Diana's mother to maintain independence and dignity. This home is a good example of aging-in-place design.

The home is our sanctuary, our refuge from the outside world. It should be an empowering place, a place that embraces us, offers us support for the activities and tasks required within its spaces, regardless of our age or ability. A house is a home when it works for life!

HOUSING BASICS

3

The home should be a personalized refuge, protection from the outside world; a place of comfort, warmth, and security.

HOUSING BASICS

WHAT STRUCTURES HAVE MORE MEANING TO US THAN OUR HOME?

Since the beginning of time man has required shelter as one of his basic needs. However that shelter means much more to us than just a place to protect us from the elements of nature. The home should be a personalized refuge, protection from the outside world; a place of comfort, warmth, and security. Whatever its style or size, whether it's urban or rural, one's place of dwelling is usually the most significant place in anyone's life.

In the beginning, people sought shelter in the forms Mother Nature provided. People dwelled in rock formations, caves, created structures from dirt, clay, and foliage. History has shown that even then, man personalized his space with pictures and decoration. People's places of dwelling have always impacted their quality of life. As man has progressed, so has the shelter.

Architectural designers are taught that the difference between architecture and a building is the intent of the designer or the meaning within the design. Vitruvius, one of history's first acknowledged architects, claimed that architecture must possess three qualities: "commodity, firmness, and delight". Commodity refers to the function, the shelter that the structure provides, protection from the elements of nature. Firmness or the form is basically the security of the structure. It must stand up against the elements and keep the occupants safe. The delight is expressed in the beauty of the structure or the meaning it conveys, similar to the feelings one experiences when interacting with art.

Most single family dwellings are not categorized as architecture, therefore many design schools across the country offer little or no specific instruction in the field of residential design. I challenge this educational approach. If meaning plays a role in the description of architecture, what structures, other than spiritual ones, have more meaning to us than our homes?

Historical evidence reveals that Native Americans dwelled in this country before the first settlers. Some were nomadic, traveling across the region using temporary housing. Others, such as the Pueblo built structures from materials found from the earth to dwell in. But since it is commonly understood that

HOUSING BASICS

the log cabin was one of the first homes built in America by the settlers, let's begin the discussion there.

The log cabin is considered vernacular architecture. Its development stemmed from the materials readily available from the land, the basic needs of the people, and the speed in which they needed shelter. Most log cabins were built with two rooms, a stone fire place, and a loft. Versions evolved with the addition of the cooking area to the rear and a detached smoke house. As soon as the saw mill for the area was up and running the log structures were clad with wooden siding and white washed to protect the logs and chinking from the elements.

Craftsmanship was crude in the early times of development. These settlers just needed shelter and protection from the environment. As the colonies prospered and adequate shelter was attained, the early "millwork," men devoted more time to architectural beauty.

Craftsmanship and detail expressed over entry.

Primitive but innovative gutter over entry door.

17

HOUSING BASICS

Similar to the log cabin, modest rural dwellings were designed and built by the homeowner or local craftsman. They were vernacular architecture evolving from the basic needs of the people and the materials readily available from the land. Stick framed structures, brick and stone houses began to develop over the landscape. Many of these rural houses exist today and it's interesting to observe how they have evolved over the years to meet the needs of the many generations. These homes were typically handed down from generation to generation; it appears each generation has made its mark.

During the years the first settlers arrived here and the colonies were being settled, architecture in Europe was quite developed. Huge decorative, stone and wooden structures created cities and estates throughout the European countryside. American estate homes and urban developments soon adopted the European Styles.

With the birth of the Industrial Revolution more and more products became available on the market. People's interest in decorations for their homes increased and the Victorian era was born. These houses were quite elaborate, some were made of brick, some of wood but all were embellished with decorative wooden details. Millwork and carpentry skills had advanced dramatically and were showcased in both the interior and exterior of these homes. Victorian women decorated with lace ruffles and many accessories creating the cluttered Victorian look. Impressions were important; the more stuff one had the more affluent they appeared. Not too different from our current society.

A grand Victorian house decorated for Christmas.

HOUSING BASICS

American architects, Greene & Greene, Gamble House, Pasadena, California.

Only the wealthy could afford to have their homes designed by architects. Others were designed and built by homeowners or carpenters. They all were designed according to the lifestyles and customs of the times. History typically focuses on lives of the affluent. These houses included kitchens away from the living areas because of odors and smoke, entries that made a grand statement and offered a parlor in close proximity for formal or less intimate guests to be entertained. Bedrooms were on the upper levels. Since men usually gathered in one space and women in another, a library or billiard room was located on the first floor.

American architects such as Charles and Henry Green and Frank Lloyd Wright focused on the art of the hand crafted. Their houses offered beautifully handcrafted details of wood and stained glass. Charles and Henry Green of Green and Green were based in California where many of their bungalow homes still stand. They are most recognized for the design of the Gamble House in Pasadena.

HOUSING BASICS

This post-war cape-cod built by my father was basic construction with no decorative elements.

Frank Lloyd Wright and his distinct styles are on display throughout the country. Sears and Roebuck Company even sold house kits from catalogues that were designed by Frank Lloyd Wright. The construction of these houses required skilled labor and a fair amount of time to build and could not meet the increasing needs of the post war families requiring housing. Thus the massed produced or "cookie cutter house" was born.

Mass produced housing stripped homes of handcrafted charm. Thousands of ranch styled, cape-cod, two-story, and multi-story single family houses sprung up across the United States.

Developers built only two or three different styled plans in the same subdivisions. Houses with little or no distinction from one another lined the streets of suburbs. This housing trend continues today, the houses are much larger, but they still tend to all look and function the same.

Critics claim that most houses built prior to the massed produced era posses more character and charm. These houses were designed and built with thoughtfulness and craft, but similar to the massed produced house, they do not work in regard to our current societal needs.

It is common for houses of the same design with little or no distinction from one another to line the streets in housing developments.

Mass produced housing stripped homes of handcrafted charm. Thousands of ranch styled, cape-cod, two-story, and multi-story single family houses sprung up across the United States.

STANDARDS FOR "TYPICAL" PEOPLE

4

STANDARDS FOR "TYPICAL" PEOPLE

As the daughter of a home builder, I have been involved with the housing industry in one form or another for most of my life. This has provided me with an understanding of the housing industry and insights as to how typical housing standards fail us.

The housing industry has formed standards or typical applications that most builders tend to adhere to. The majority of the population is of average size and physical ability, this typical category has set the standards for residential design. Hallways have typically been 36" wide, (most interior doors range from 26" to 32" wide), and the majority of bathrooms are 5' by 7' to accommodate the standard 5' wide bathtub, 36" vanity, and the toilet. These standards create difficulty for anyone with special needs but also make it harder to maneuver furniture in and out of spaces, or to pass someone in the hallway.

This represents a typical bedroom and bathroom plan: a 36" hallway, 28" to 32" door openings, small closets and standard 5' wide bathrooms.

These "standards" and "typicals" hinder the functional aspects of the way we should be able to dwell in our homes.

When I asked my father why hallways were only 36" wide, he claimed that, "In my forty-five years of experience, homeowners just wouldn't pay the additional cost for wider hallways."

Well if that's the case, we should design houses without hallways or make these transitional spaces so interesting that people would be willing to pay for the additional space.

Throughout history, houses have been designed by homeowners, builders, residential designers, and architects; however, only the affluent homeowner could afford to have a home custom designed by a professional designer.

Developers and builders have concentrated on mass marketing production and budget instead of striving to create well designed homes. People are accustomed to typical house designs and, unless they have experienced a special situation, give little thought about what they might require from a house in the future or if their current situation changes due to an illness or accident. This attitude

STANDARDS FOR "TYPICAL" PEOPLE

> A program consists of collecting and analyzing information obtained through research and interviews, documentation of that information and stating the design problem.

of the developers and buyers has resulted in an influx of poorly designed buildings that house people, buildings that offer shelter and little else in the category of function. Of course the expected amenities of newer homes are included, the decorative elements, luxurious bathrooms, and well equipped kitchens; but from a functional aspect they typically fail.

Designing a home is probably the most difficult design problem any designer can face. When designing public spaces for the general population, majority rules, but when we design intimate places for personal use we must consider each user individually. This makes it quite difficult to design houses for the market. When designing a market house the program development deals more with demographics and general market research. A client profile must be created for the desired price range. This preliminary work takes many hours of research and development before the design begins, but proves well worth with when the final project is complete.

Designing a home for a client allows the opportunity for exploration of their lifestyle, wants, needs and dreams for the future. A program is developed and followed throughout the project insuring that the needs of a particular family are met. This takes time and strong communication skills. Quite often a husband and wife will have different ideas about what they would like in their home. It is the designer's responsibility to find a solution that pleases everyone. I often joke about my job being half designer and half marriage counselor. Even though designing for clients can be difficult at times, it is still easier than designing a house for the general market.

> I often joke about my job being half designer and half marriage counselor.

STANDARDS FOR "TYPICAL" PEOPLE

Good residential designers should do the research and understand universal or inclusive design concepts as well as sustainable design theories and applications. Once educated in these areas, the typical, standard residential design practices no longer make sense. As the population ages and the needs for this population change, the housing industry will be forced to change with it. Residential designers will be required to have the knowledge and the skills to meet this new demand.

STANDARD HOUSE TYPES

The following are basic standard plan typologies of the single family house. In different regions the sizes and styles of these floor-plans may vary, but basically they are all quite similar. I am providing this information so you may identify what type of house in which you reside. Some of these typologies are easier to renovate and make work than others, but I can assure you that I have been challenged by all of these and successful solutions were achieved.

Not all ranches enter from the ground level, this ranch has several steps up to the front door and the garage enters from the basement level.

THE RANCH OR SINGLE FLOOR PLAN

Ranch styled homes during the post war phase were much smaller than newer versions, ranging from 800 to 1,700 square feet. These plans are one level with the front door usually entering directly into the living area without any distinction from the rest of the room. The kitchen and dining spaces are to the rear of the plan with a hallway to the bedrooms and bath coming off the main living space. Two to three bedrooms were common, the bedrooms being quite tight with small closets. If the house was built with a basement that's typically where the utilities and laundry were located.

STANDARDS FOR "TYPICAL" PEOPLE

Many of these houses were built on a slab or crawl space for cost effectiveness. In this situation the utilities and laundry were located in a small room usually off the kitchen near the garage, if a garage existed. These houses were simple in form. They were a basic rectangle with a straight gable roof. Most only provided a concrete stoop or slab at the location of the front door without any type of roof over it. They were cost effective and easily constructed.

Today, the single floor dwelling has evolved into complex forms with complicated roof lines. The basic rectangle has given way to all kinds of shapes. Vaulted ceilings and hipped roofs have become the standard. The total square footage has increased dramatically. This type of house per square foot is the most costly.

Typical ranch plan.

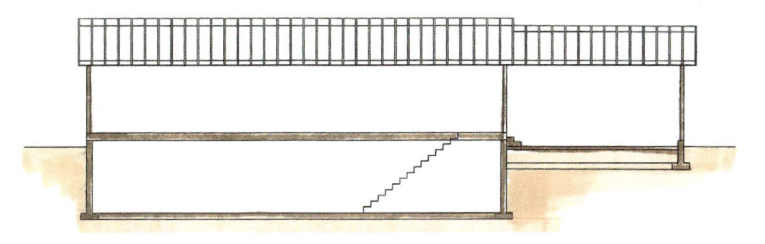

Typical ranch section.

STANDARDS FOR "TYPICAL" PEOPLE

THE **CAPE-COD** OR 1-1/2 STORY

Large cape-cod of the 1950's & 1960's. A wide dormer is located on the back of this house.

The cape-cod styled house is basically the ranch with a higher pitched roof so the bedrooms could be located on a second level within the roof structure. Dormers were added to the roof line to allow for the windows. This creates very interesting spaces on the second floor. The ceilings slope down to meet short walls and the dormers form irregular shaped rooms. Most have one bedroom and bathroom on the first floor along with a kitchen, dining area, and living room. The large space of the second floor may be divided by the staircase. In larger cape-cods a second bathroom could be an option upstairs. Like the ranch, the utilities and laundry are typically in the basement unless the house was built on a crawl space or slab, then they were located off the kitchen.

Many cape-cods have a garage connected with a breezeway to the main house. This house used to be cheaper than a typical two-story because the second floor is housed within the attic space, but due to current construction codes this type of house has become quite costly to construct. Today's plans are much larger, but it is still a popular plan for a custom home and looks great in a country setting. Not too many are being built in the mass- produced market.

STANDARDS FOR "TYPICAL" PEOPLE

Typical cape-cod plan.

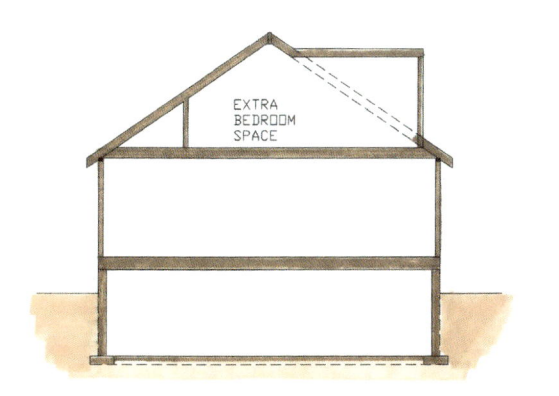

Typical cape-cod section.

THE **TWO-STORY** HOUSE

Older two story houses are typically four rooms on the first floor and four rooms up with utilities and laundry in the basement. The first floor consists of, the living room with entry and staircase to the front of the plan and the kitchen and dining room to the rear. Most have a half bath under the staircase off the entry hall. The second floor offers three bedrooms with small closets and a bathroom. The basement, if provided, houses the utilities and laundry. Later it became popular for the laundry to be located near the kitchen serving as the family entry and mud room. Most two stories offer a basement and the staircase to the basement is placed directly under the staircase to the upstairs.

The two story house is extremely popular due to its cost effectiveness and ease to build, when spaces are squarely stacked on top of each other and mechanicals and plumbing line up from floor to floor, square footage cost decrease.

The new two-story shows up in housing developments everywhere. It has become common for living areas or great rooms to be two stories high with overlooking balconies from the second floor. The entries also tower into the second floor space leaving volumes of cubic footage to heat and cool.

STANDARDS FOR "TYPICAL" PEOPLE

Older two-story home.

People admire these spaces upon first impression, but they soon realize they are not real comfortable for everyday life. Sounds echo throughout the spaces, privacy on the second floor is compromised, and the space is out of proportion with human scale. Furniture must be oversized to look right, and window treatments and ventilation control most often have to be operated by remote. These market houses are popular and comprise the majority of the market houses being offered.

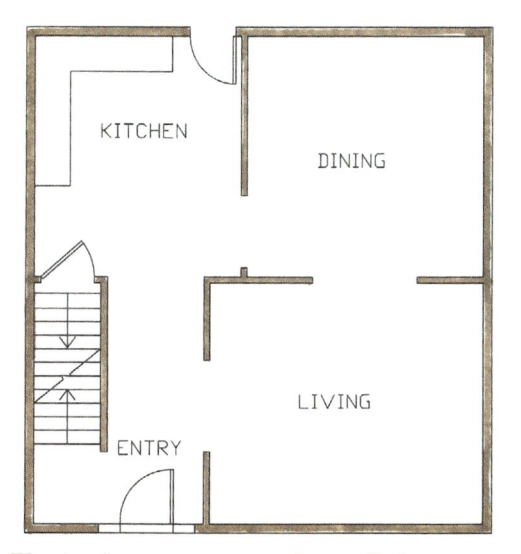

STANDARDS FOR "TYPICAL" PEOPLE

Typical two-story plan of the past.

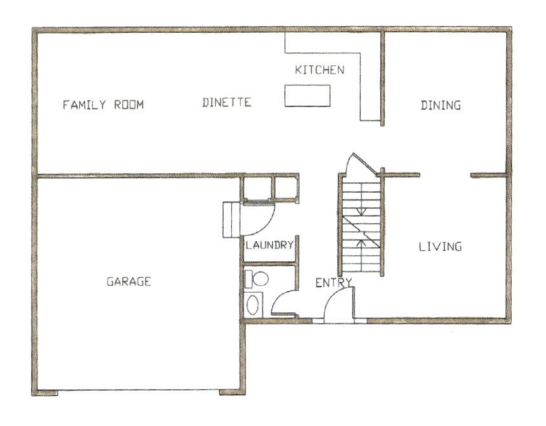

Typical two-story plan of the present.

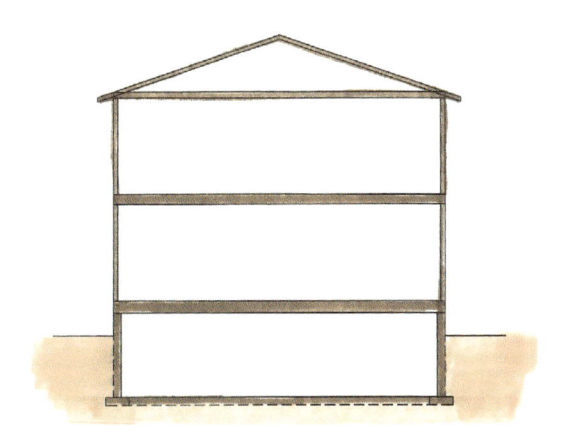

Typical two-story section.

Over the last ten years of my design practice more and more people are requesting human scaled houses, houses that make sense for energy efficiency. The two story house is still popular but changes are evolving. Vaulted living spaces are still desired but at lower heights and a first floor owner's suite is becoming standard.

STANDARDS FOR "TYPICAL" PEOPLE

THE **BI-LEVEL** OR SPLIT-LEVEL HOUSE

Bi-level with attached garage.

The bi-level is similar to a two story but the lower floor is halfway below grade level and the second floor is halfway above grade level. The entry is on grade or a few steps up and has a staircase that goes up to the main floor and a staircase that descends to the lower floor. The upper floor typically consists of the kitchen, dining room, living room and one or two bedrooms and a bathroom. The lower level includes the family room, additional bedrooms, utilities, laundry, and usually a second bathroom. This type of house does not offer a typical basement, the lower level is usually built on a slab.

The square footage cost of this house style is one of the lowest due to the fact that the basement level has been raised halfway out of the ground and is being used as living space. The down side of this style is all of the steps. Upon entry one is forced to climb up or descend down one of the staircases to enter any kind of living space at all. Only the entry hall is on grade level.

This house type is one of the most difficult to make work for everyone. To get to either level requires traversing a staircase. Additions should have internal access from the existing structure. The new ground floor space lands between levels, resulting in an additional vertical transition.

STANDARDS FOR "TYPICAL" PEOPLE

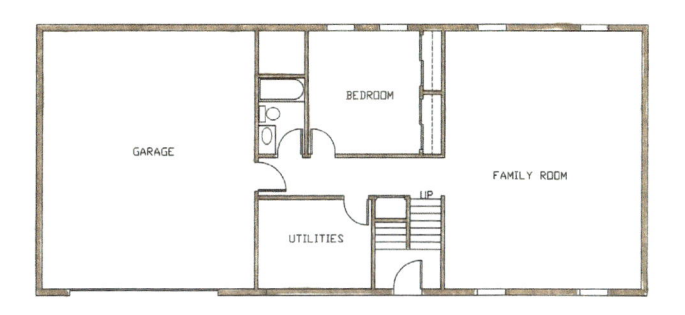

Typical bi-level lower level plan.

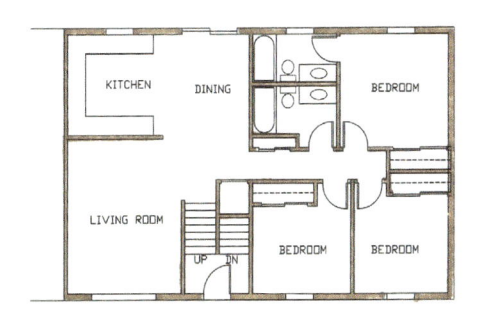

Typical bi-level upper level plan.

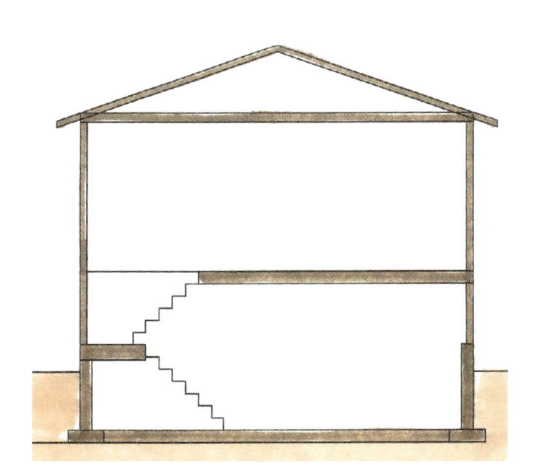

Typical bi-level section.

I recently worked with clients living in a bi-level and wished to have the wife's parents reside with them in their home. Her parent's health was beginning to deteriorate and they knew the space provided for them must be accessible. We were able to attach a completely accessible living quarters onto the side of their home in a manner that actually improved the aesthetic of their house. The addition incorporated ground level living quarters, entry and a garage. The interior connection to the existing house was created by extending the hallway on the upper level that led to a staircase located in the addition.

STANDARDS FOR "TYPICAL" PEOPLE

THE TRI-LEVEL
OR MULTI-LEVEL HOUSE

Large Tri-level with attached garage.

The tri-level offers three floors with the main level on grade, a lower level halfway below grade, and an upper level over the lower level which is halfway above grade. The kitchen, dining area, and living room are on the main floor level. Sometimes the garage is also located on this level and entered into from the kitchen/dinette space. In this situation the family room is in the lower level. Another version offers the garage in the lower level with a family room off the kitchen. All bedrooms and bathrooms are located in the highest level.

Multi-level houses come in a variety of plans. Most are similar to the tri-level but offer addition space in a basement level under the main level of the house.

After living in a tri-level for a few years in my early childhood I began to wonder why the tri-level was such a big seller in the 60s and 70s. My father must have built and sold a hundred of them. He claimed the tri-level provided the most house for the money, and price per square footage is what sells.

STANDARDS FOR "TYPICAL" PEOPLE

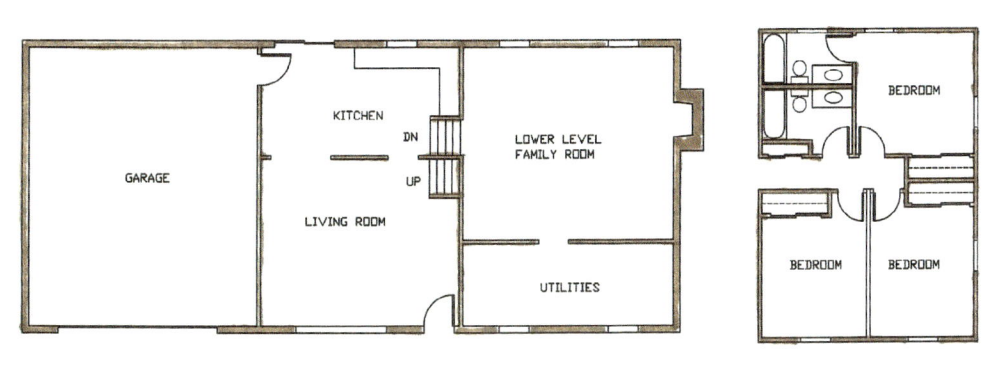

Typical tri-level plan.

upper level.

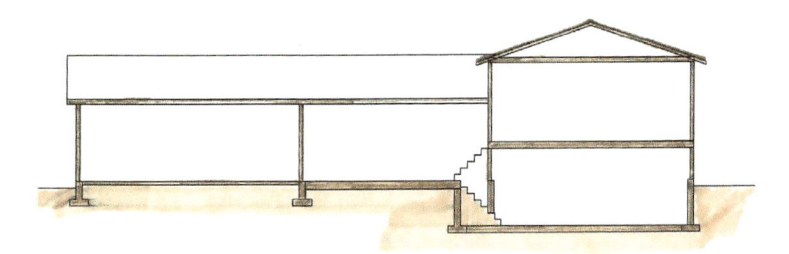

Typical bi-level section.

Over the years I have designed many additions for tri-level homes allowing easier access to an owner's suite, bath and laundry.

STANDARDS FOR "TYPICAL" PEOPLE

THE URBAN HOUSE

This home represents a typical house in urban developments. This image is of a newer home based on historic Greek Revival Architecture. These homes are long and narrow usually offering the living room, dining room and kitchen on the first floor with bedrooms and bathrooms located on the upper floors.

Urban three-story home. Lisa's brother's house.

This particular house belongs to my brother. When he was fifty-six years old and assumingly in perfect health, he was out shopping with a friend and suddenly became extremely ill. Within hours he was admitted into the hospital with a severe case of pancreatitis. He was not released from the hospital for nearly three months. He had been in bed without any exercise for ten weeks before he was well enough for physical therapy. As the time for his release approached the doctor and nurse in charge began asking questions about his house. It was determined he could not negotiate the stairs in his physical condition and would not be released without the assurance that he had another place to go with a first floor bedroom and bath. Luckily my mother had just moved into a condo. It was not completely accessible but the use of a wheelchair was not required. My brother was just too weak to climb steps. Another three months passed before he was strong enough to return to his home.

STANDARDS FOR "TYPICAL" PEOPLE

Many of us live in denial and think nothing like this could ever happen to us, my brother included. He designed and built this home without considering the need for a first floor bedroom or elevator. When things like this happen it may be impossible to make the revisions required quick enough to return home. In this case, it is not feasible to revise this house to accommodate a physically disabled person. The lot is too narrow for additional first floor space, the existing spaces can not be converted and an elevator would have too negative of an impact on the existing spaces of the home.

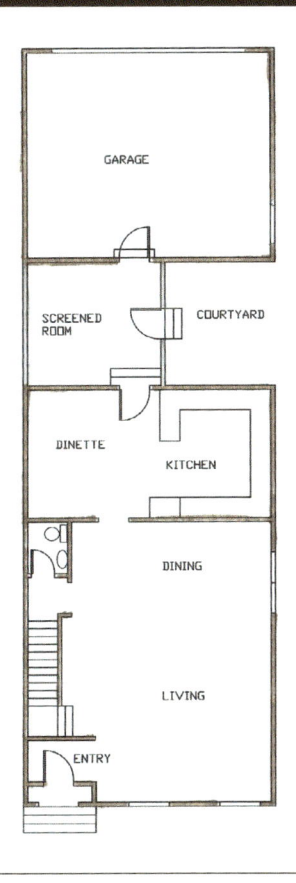

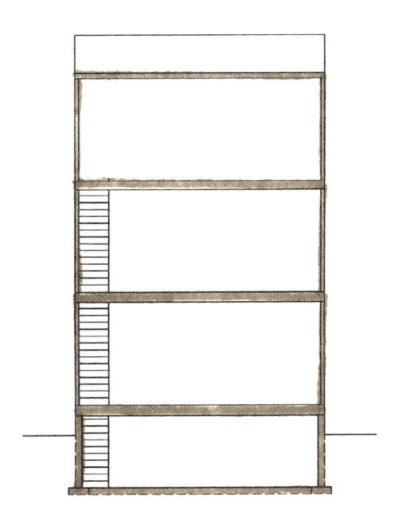

Urban three-story plan and section

THE SITE – Orientation, Topography and Context

5

Often the views from the inside or the views to the exterior are "overlooked".

THE SITE - ORIENTATION, TOPOGRAPHY AND CONTEXT

Site evaluation is a major element with any well designed house. Too often, even expensive homes are built with no consideration to the attributes or deficiencies of the site. How the house relates to the site, its orientation to the sun, the lay of the land and the surrounding environment are critical to a successful design. Often the views from the inside or the views to the exterior are "overlooked".

Example of "cookie cutter house" on rural lot.

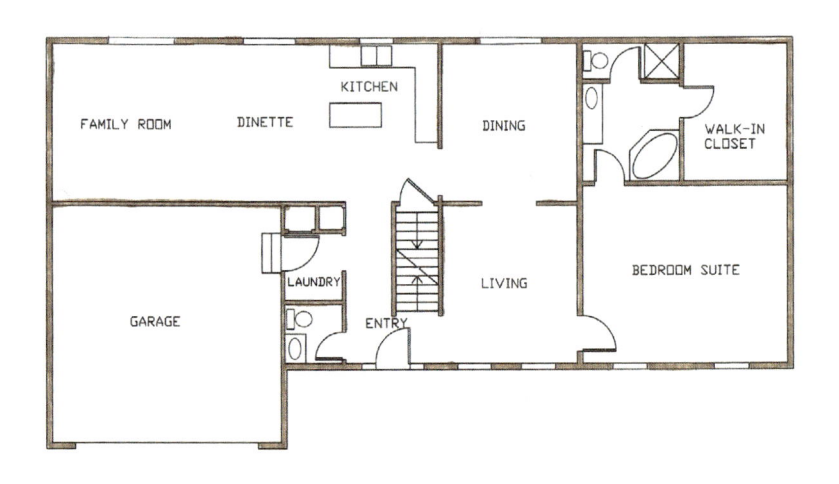

The view out the back of this house is amazing but the plan does not address it well.

Houses that are not designed specifically for their site are noticeable to even to the untrained eye. This is evident with many newer houses built in rural areas. Even though these houses sit on sites that are wider than subdivision lots allowing ample room for the driveway to traverse around the house to an inconspicuously located garage door, the garages still boldly face the road. The front elevation expresses all of the architectural interest leaving the side and rear elevations flat and uninteresting. It is easy to see

THE SITE - ORIENTATION, TOPOGRAPHY AND CONTEXT

that these house plans are mass produced and offered in catalogues for Anywhere, USA.

When attention is given to the different aspects a site can offer, the design can be engaging from all vantage points. Lower level spaces may open up to interesting outdoor areas, houses that appear to be one level may actually be two levels from another vantage point. The orientation of the site dictates the way natural light enters at different times of the day dramatically enhancing the interior space. Sunrooms on the south façade are really sunrooms, capturing the warmth of the south sun on cold winter days.

A house that actually relates to its site, whether it claims the site, evolves from the earth, or blends in, may add to the experience of dwelling. Houses that claim the site might be perched on a hill with a commanding view of the surrounding area. Other houses might appear to be growing from the land. These homes have a lower level that is partially exposed and partially within the earth. A house that blends in, usually sits within the landscape, it may be surrounded by earth and foliage.

Outdoor places are just as important as indoor spaces and should be incorporated for a successful design. When we don't fully understand what the site has to offer, it is impossible to create outdoor spaces that provide privacy, the right amount of sunlight, or views. Most of us prefer to be outdoors when the weather permits. An outdoor room can be the perfect spot to enjoy fresh air and sunshine or rest in the coolness of shade.

Where you choose to live, either in a rural, urban or suburban setting may be determined by budget, proximity to employment, personal and philosophical preference, or a combination of all. Many people are moving into the city due to monetary reasons or to be closer to their job, some

THE SITE - ORIENTATION, TOPOGRAPHY AND CONTEXT

to reduce their carbon footprint. We may choose a rural setting for the privacy it provides or for the opportunity to "get off the grid". Others still prefer the lifestyle a subdivision offers. Whatever your choice, most will agree that the movement to be "green" is growing in leaps and bounds and affecting the decisions we make.

"Green" is a relative term. I like to consider all of its shades. The shades range from what I refer to as Mother Nature green to the color of money green with a multitude of shades in between. Mother Nature is a true green, the most earth friendly. At the other end of the spectrum is the shade of money; this green is the most deceiving. Many industries are misleading consumers to buy goods that fall in the shade of money category. The green movement has become a huge money maker and not all products are created with the Mother Nature shade of green in mind. This topic is complex and might require another book to fully explain.

There are a multitude of resources for you to investigate and help you in your decision making process. Information is available in print and online. One thing to remember is that the only answer to any question regarding a product's rating of sustainability is it depends. There are so many variables to consider; its life cost, carbon footprint, toxicity to produce and the list goes on. Just be aware of the products you buy and try your best to make the right decisions for you.

THE SITE - ORIENTATION, TOPOGRAPHY AND CONTEXT

1. Chicken Pen
2. Barn
3. Pool
4. Grape Arbor
5. Raised Garden Beds
6. Orchard
7. Spa
8. East Patio
9. Planter/Retaining Wall
10. Basement Egress
11. Fire Pit
12. Patio
13. Grill Area
14. Garden Bed
15. Fish Pond & Waterfall
16. Covered Porch
17. Covered Entry
18. Ramped Concrete Walkway
19. Planter/Wall
20. Parking
21. Drive
22. Drive to Additional Acerage
23. Geothermal Loop System
24. Wood Fencing

The site offers many opportunities to be green and enhance your quality of life. This is a diagram of my residence; it has evolved over many years of personalizing, renovating and striving to be eco-friendly.

THE SITE - ORIENTATION, TOPOGRAPHY AND CONTEXT

ENERGY EFFICIENCY

We can always be comforted by knowing that we are consuming as little energy as possible from both an environmental and economic perspective. The site plays an important role in energy consumption and the options that are available. North, east, south and west in relationship to your home and its planning effects how well your house will work from an energy standpoint. Solar technology is advancing at a dramatic pace but south exposure will most likely remain critical for its use. The north-west side of most houses will take the brunt of a harsh winter climate and the east will provide morning light.

Current technology is rapidly changing, but at the time of this publication one of the best ways to achieve energy efficiency is by use of a geothermal heating and cooling system. Geothermal systems extract the energy from the earth to heat and cool your home. The process may also provide hot water. The method of installation depends on the type of lot the house sits on. A loop system is used when enough space is available; on small lots wells need to be drilled. Geothermal systems are becoming very popular but often quite expensive. It would be a good idea to talk to a local professional for more information about the energy options available in your area.

Even if you live in a newer home you should still double check the basics concerning energy efficiency. Make sure your home has proper levels of insulation, energy efficient windows, resists air infiltration, and clean furnace and air conditioning filters. Replace inefficient light bulbs with efficient ones, turn lights and appliances off when not needed and unplug chargers when not in use.

THE SITE - ORIENTATION, TOPOGRAPHY AND CONTEXT

I recently had the privilege of designing a renovation and addition for clients that desired to live in a home that qualified as a perma-culture homestead. This earth friendly philosophy incorporates man with nature in a very profound way. The site consists of over twenty acres of fairly undeveloped land. A large creek pierces one side of the meadow valley which is surrounded by trees. The clients required a passive solar, energy efficient home and used as many "green" materials as possible. The program was extensive and included a variety of future contingencies and options. Eventually when the technology advances, they wish to install solar panels, harvest the hydro energy from the creek and collect the energy from the wind that consistently blows through the valley. The orientation to the sun, the structural form of the addition, and what spaces would be maintained in the existing structure, all were factors in the success of the design. Their current lifestyle, existing furniture and dreams for the future were also addressed.

All in all, the project was a success with many attributes. The house is energy efficient. It takes advantage of south facing insulated windows, thermal massing, extra insulation, and has a geothermal system. The existing house works well as the private areas of the home with the addition serving as the public spaces.

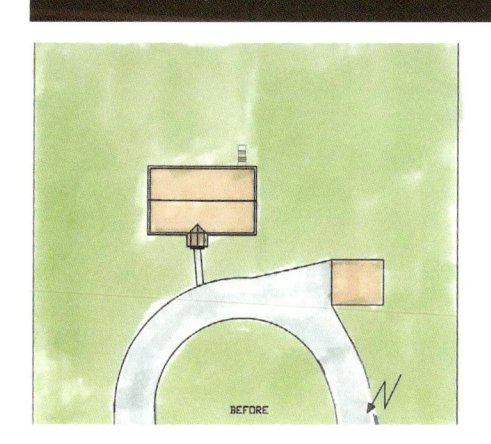

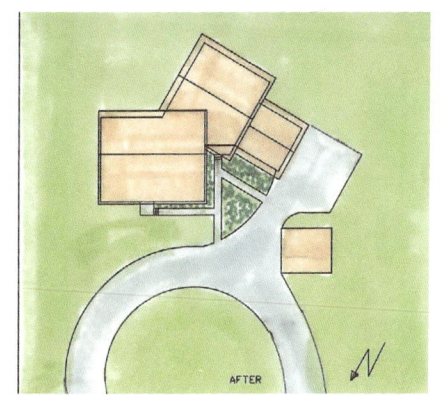

BEFORE

AFTER

Original house was a basic ranch with a covered front porch. The addition was rotated 30 degrees to face due south. The roof structure was designed to receive solar panels. Addition works as a passive solar space taking advantage of the sun for warmth, shade and air flow for cooling. The entry was relocated to incorporate a courtyard and landscaping. The car port was added to provide a covered entry and assimilate the existing garage into the composition.

THE SITE - ORIENTATION, TOPOGRAPHY AND CONTEXT

How your house is placed on its site dramatically effects how well your home will work. Consider all of the features of the land, both negative and positive in the design or renovation of your home. Address the negatives as challenges to be solved and the positives as attributes to be relished. Dwelling is not just about the inside of the house, it is about the site as well.

"Permaculture (permanent agriculture) is the harmonious integration of landscape and people providing their food, energy, shelter, and other material and non-material needs in a sustainable way. It is also the conscious design and maintenance of agriculturally productive ecosystems which have the diversity, stability and resilience of natural ecosystems."

PUBLIC AND PRIVATE LIVING

6

Due to the nature of dwelling, or how we live within a structure, houses have always had designated public spaces, private spaces and spaces in between.

PUBLIC AND PRIVATE LIVING

Designers are taught to create with a concept driving the design process. A good concept usually results in a good design. The public versus private concept is known to most designers. Throughout my education and teaching career the use of this concept was explored by many interior design and architectural students for a variety of building types. Developing a concept for a residential project is extremely difficult because a home is such a personal space, but I have found the public vs. private concept to be most effective in the field of residential design. When followed, it makes sense with most people's lifestyles.

Due to the nature of dwelling, or how we live within a structure, houses have always had designated public spaces, private spaces and spaces in between. If we explore this concept further we find that the most private family spaces are sometimes used by the public (visitors) and public spaces are often used by the residents of the home. The kitchen is considered a semi-private space. It is typically used by the people who live in the home but it is often shared with extended family and friends. A bathroom that is located in the private sector of the home could be used by any visitor if the need arises. The transition spaces, the areas where we move from one space to another, can also be identified within this concept. The foyer or front entry hall is a public space. The family entry is usually private. The bedroom wing is a private space but the transition space to this area could also be the path to a guest bath or bedroom.

Interior designers specialize in space planning. This includes space adjacencies and sequences of space. The functional aspects of the home, or the activities and uses of the spaces being designed, should be thoroughly studied and explored. We need to consider all users' current and future requirements and the public versus private concept. By doing this, we can achieve a house design that really makes sense for the way people want to live. The house can "work for life!"

In a typical house, little, if any attention is given to the public versus private concept and the experience of dwelling is negatively affected. The great room or main living area is often within full view of the front entry. If the great room is the only space provided for family interaction, conversation, or just the place to hang out and watch TV, privacy is compromised when a complete stranger comes to the front door. The family's private activities are no longer private. In a two-story, it is common for staircase to the upstairs to land in the formal entry hall. This staircase is an architectural feature that

PUBLIC AND PRIVATE LIVING

This entry welcomes visitors but keeps private areas of the home secluded.

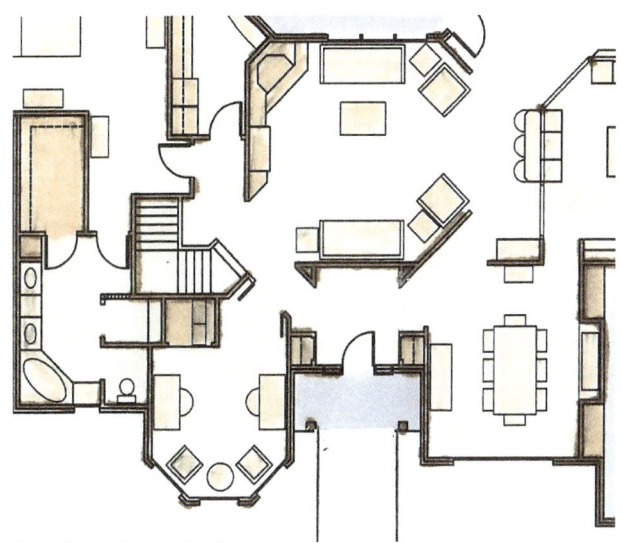

Plan view of opposite image.

most want to show off, so there it is, in the most public space of the home. But when we really consider the function of this staircases and where it leads, it doesn't make sense to have the path to the most private areas of the house exposed to the most public space. Should our children have to pass the front door when they want a drink of water during the night? Wouldn't it make more sense to have the landing of this staircase in a private area of the house? A portion of the stair could still be exposed to the entry to be admired by the guests entering and leaving the home, but by the guests entering and leaving the home, I have discovered that that when the family has visual access from the private zone, it is very much appreciated.

Another common feature in some two-story house designs is a view into the kitchen from the front entry. This public exposure of a semi-private and often messy area of the home is not so desirable. Our entry should give a good impression, be welcoming and inviting. A sink full of dirty dishes might not be the impression we want to give to the unexpected visitor.

51

PUBLIC AND PRIVATE LIVING

Direct view into the kitchen is common in many two-story homes. This home does not offer a drop zone, so everything ends up on the kitchen island. Note the staircase in main entry.

PUBLIC AND PRIVATE LIVING

When we consider this basic concept of public spaces, private spaces and all spaces in between, we can create places that make sense with the way we really prefer to live.

CREATING HOUSES THAT *WORK FOR LIFE!*

7

As cultural and societal criteria evolve, so does the house.

CREATING HOUSES THAT WORK FOR LIFE

As designers we are trained to truly see the built environment around us, to look at the world with a critical eye, and explore better ways to create space. This approach allows us to achieve the goal of improving the built environment. The practice of post occupancy evaluation also helps designers reach this goal. Post occupancy evaluation is the process of extensive research evaluating a building's performance after its completion. Designers study usage patterns and conduct informing interviews with the building's occupants. Without this evaluation process we can only assume what we are designing is working. This practice is virtually non-existent in residential design but should be included in every design process.

Educators of design students teach through constructive criticism. This critiquing system has become a part of my everyday life. It is difficult for me to enter someone's home without trying to find better ways for the house to work.

While on a women's outing, we visited an older quad-level home that was well kept and quite nice. All of the women were impressed with the newlywed's house and their redecorating accomplishments. I, on the other hand, noticed how small the bathrooms were and wondered how an overweight person could even fit through the extremely narrow doorway. The bathrooms were located up a staircase that offered no handrails for support and I observed how difficult it was for my friend with bad knees to make her way up the steps. My friends and I are not considered elders yet, but many of us have conditions that make the standard home unsafe and difficult for us to maneuver. I was concerned that many of the neighboring houses of similar designs were occupied by the elder population and wondered how safely and comfortably they were aging in this type of house.

CREATING HOUSES THAT WORK FOR LIFE

As cultural and societal criteria evolve, so does the house. The bathroom located in the owner's or master's suite of the average market house is quite glamorous compared to the bathrooms of the sixties and seventies. The gathering spaces are grander and the kitchens are designed for the gourmet chef. But does all of this extravagance make these spaces function any better? To a certain degree they do, for the typical, able bodied user for whom the current market is targeted. These amenities are appreciated and may enhance our life as long as we stay within the typical target market. But most of these homes do not work for the many, through aging, illness or accidents that no longer qualify as typical. By implementing a different design strategy and approach to the market, all houses could function better for all users.

Every space in a house has been developed around an activity or task. The space is commonly described by its usage: the living room, bathroom, laundry room, bedroom, you get the idea. These rooms are spaces designated for certain activities to take place within the home. The following section takes an in-depth look at the many spaces and places that make up a home. These descriptive guidelines and examples will assist us in creating houses that work for life.

CREATING HOUSES THAT WORK FOR LIFE

CREATING HOUSES THAT WORK FOR LIFE

THE ENTRIES

GUEST ENTRY

The purpose of the front or guest entry is for visitors or residents to transition from the exterior to the interior of a house or vice versa.

The exterior entry areas of most houses consist of a walkway, steps, landing or porch, sometimes covered and sometimes not, and an entry door. Once we cross the threshold and have arrived inside, we are often greeted with a direct view of the private living spaces of the home. If the house is a two-story, the staircase is usually located in this entry, thus inviting the guests up into the most private sector of the house, the upstairs bedrooms. Staircases are great architectural features and offer beauty and drama to the entry, but when applying the public vs. private concept, this location makes little sense. Many two-story houses also provide a direct view into the kitchen from the front door area, again, compromising the privacy of a semi-private sector. The kitchen is also a work place and might not always offer the best image to our guest, like dirty dishes in the sink, or a cluttered countertop.

It is common for older homes to offer no transition or entry space at all. Sometimes the front door opens directly into the living area without any delineation from the rest of the room. The flooring may be different, and a half wall might divide the space, but the view to the family's living area is wide open.

Many moderately priced homes of the 50's and 60's have front doors that open directly into a living space.

CREATING HOUSES THAT WORK FOR LIFE

VISITABLE

All houses should strive to be at least visit-able. This term is fairly new to the housing industry and refers to the minimal requirements of an accessible or step-less entry and one accessible bathroom. If all houses were visit-able, the elder and physically challenged population would be included in the everyday activities of our society instead of being excluded from one of the basic privileges of being a guest in someone's home.

Houses that work for life should provide a slightly sloped or step-less walkway beautifully landscaped with raised flower beds flanking it. The walkway should offer ample lighting, be generous in width and the surface material even and slip proof. It should lead to a well illuminated covered place, where one can anticipate being invited into the home while being protected from inclement weather.

The current building codes in most areas of the United States require a minimum of eight inches of exposed foundation above the grade or earth level. This provides protection against the damaging invasion of termites but it poses problems with accessible entries into the home. When we raise the foundation eight inches, and place the floor structure on the concrete foundation walls, we have created an interior floor level that is at least three steps above the ground surrounding the house. An effective method to reduce the level change from exterior to interior is to notch the foundation wall. This provides a lower surface to receive the floor joist. You will still have a level change, but it will be reduced with this construction method.

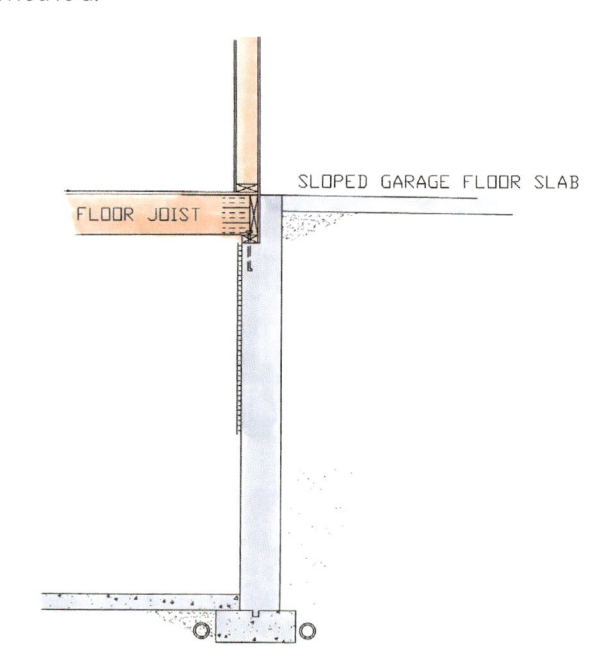

We have all seen houses with ramps built of decking material or steel added onto the front of someone's home. This is a sure sign that someone that lives in the house or visits is physically challenged and requires the use of a wheelchair.

CREATING HOUSES THAT WORK FOR LIFE

Universal or inclusive design strives to achieve equal treatment for everyone, the able bodied and disabled, without stigmatizing anyone. When a ramp is evident on the front of one's home, it announces to the world that someone different lives there. This can have a profound effect on one's psychological well being.

If someone in your household or a close family member requires the use of a wheelchair, could they safely and independently live in or visit your home? Most likely not, but this requirement is becoming more and more common in our society as the baby-boomer generation ages and people with disabilities desire a "normal" lifestyle.

By addressing these needs while designing, renovating, and building our homes, we can avoid the problems. Concrete can be easily ramped at a slight slope to permit the physically challenged population to enter our homes safely, without the difficulties that steps pose. With creative landscape design and some preliminary research, all houses can be made accessible in an attractive manner. Ramped walkways can be landscaped with earth and plantings or flanked with stone or brick planters to disguise the slope and enhance the house's appearance. Drainage issues might arise and should be addressed prior to construction, so it is important to let your designer and builder know that you want a ramped walkway before the project begins.

The main entry should be noticeable and make a statement on the front of the house. This provides a visual clue to guests that this is the door they should enter. Some designers in the past have toyed with this idea; Frank Lloyd Wright was notorious for hiding the main entry and making the visitor explore the forms of the house before they discovered the place to enter. From a functional standpoint, this way of entering might be quite an inconvenience for some people, especially if it were pouring down rain and they couldn't find the front door. In Frank Lloyd Wright's defense, his houses had such large protruding overhangs most of the walkways were covered.

If someone in your houshold or a close family member requires the use of a wheelchair, could they safely and independently live in or visit your home?

CREATING HOUSES THAT WORK FOR LIFE

> *I find it very disturbing to see a front door without any type of protection over it. Many market houses, especially two-stories, do not offer this feature. It not only looks better when a front door is emphasized with a roof, it makes functional sense as well. A covered entry protects people and the front door from the elements. But when the budget is driving the design, as it often does, this feature is unfortunately sacrificed.*

Lighting is another important element, both functionally and aesthetically. Homes should provide a safe and secure feeling to residents and guests alike. Illumination of the walkways, the entry door, and the address signage, provides safe passage and security to the visitor that they are at the right house.

Once we have entered into the home only glimpses of the private area beyond should be in view. In a two-story home, the beauty of a grand staircase leading to the private areas may be appreciated without offering direct access to the upper and most private level of the house. A formal dining area, formal living room, music room, or office may flank the entry but the private living areas should be discretely located further inside the house. A closet or hall tree for guest coat storage near the front door is a must. A beautiful piece of furniture with a decorative mirror enhances the aesthetics of the space, but it may also improve the functional aspects as well. The furniture could provide extra storage for guest's belongings and the mirror gives one the opportunity for a brief check of their appearance before greeting the visitors or leaving the house.

The foyer or entry hall makes the first and last impression of your home to visitors and guests. It should be designed with features that make a good impression of your home with a touch of your family's personality expressed. Unique architectural features such as a barrel vault, niches, columns, and moldings add interest and charm. Foyers that have been designed to display antique pieces of furniture, artwork, and family heirlooms double as a gallery and can really create a wonderful experience for all that enter and leave the space.

CREATING HOUSES THAT WORK FOR LIFE

The barrel vault is an effective way to enhance the entry's architectural interest; the columns screen the family area from visitor's view.

Foyer or Guest Entry should include:

Exterior
- A wide, illuminated walkway with an even and slip resistant surface
- A step-less, accessible entry, 36" minimum door
- Illuminated address sign
- Illuminated covered waiting area
- An architectural emphasis that makes an impression

Interior
- Interesting architectural details
- Mirror
- Guest coat storage
- Easily maintained flooring
- Adjacency to public spaces
- Distance from private spaces

CREATING HOUSES THAT WORK FOR LIFE

FAMILY ENTRY

The back door or family entry is the most important entry of the house. It is where the residents of the home come and go. The home is our sanctuary from the outside world and the experience of entering and leaving it should be welcoming and pleasant. All too often, this space includes the laundry facilities or is a mud room forcing us to pass through dirty clothes or a cluttered catch-all space, offering little or no aesthetic pleasure as we come and go from our homes. As we leave or return to our homes we should never be burdened with the reminder of undone chores. The space should make us feel happy to be home or leave us with the feelings of support and encouragement as we depart.

This area of our home should empower us, aid us in the organization of our lives and help us make life easier. This entry, usually adjacent to the garage, is where we carry in and out all of the necessities of everyday life; the groceries, dry cleaning, mail, and other miscellaneous supplies. The location of this entry should always be near the kitchen, where most of the supplies are needed. We should never have to schlep groceries from one side or level of the house to another.

It is crucial to have a landing place for all the stuff we carry into our homes. I call this place "the drop zone". When a drop zone is not provided, the mail, briefcases and book bags end up on the kitchen counter creating uncontrollable clutter. Most of us can relate to this situation.

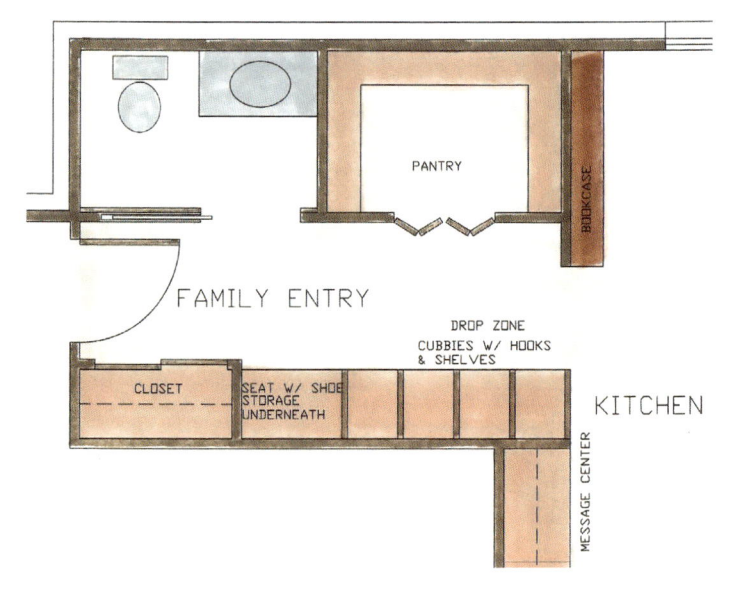

This entry serves the family well: accessible half bath, large pantry, personal storage for each member, place to sit, shoe storage, coat storage, adjacency to kitchen and message center.

CREATING HOUSES THAT WORK FOR LIFE

In a house that works, the family entry area should include a place for the family's shoes, boots, and coats, a shelf for brief-cases, or individual cubbies for book-bags, a sorting area for the mail, and a place to sit, allowing the removal and placement of shoes to be safe and easy. A window seat works great in these spaces; it provides a seat, storage, and natural light, which always makes a place better. In homes where extremely soiled shoes and boots often need to be cleaned, it is a good idea to install a shower basin with a water spigot in the bottom of the closet. This mini shower also provides a great place to rinse off the pet's paws.

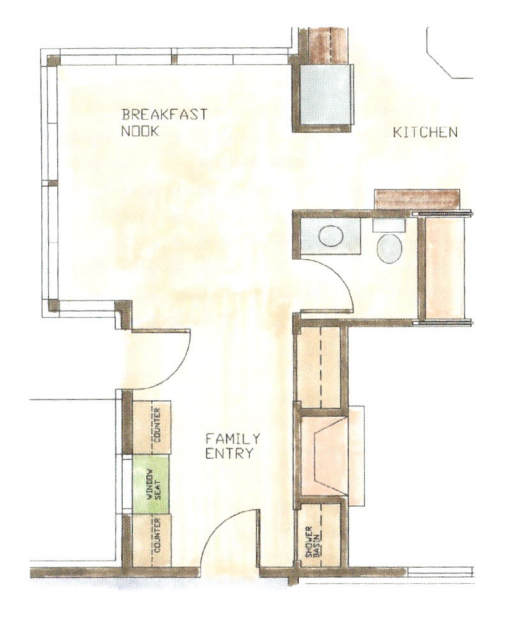

This family entry provides a shower basin in the closet for muddy boots and pet paws, a window seat, drop zone, storage and ½ bath.

It is important that this entry enters into the private zone of the home and is personalized to meet each family's individual needs. When the budget permits, it works really well to have a half-bath located near this space. Since the kitchen is nearby, the convenience of a large walk-in pantry is always appreciated.

Similar to the front entry, this transition from the garage to the interior of the house usually requires a level change. Most residential building codes dictate a minimum

CREATING HOUSES THAT WORK FOR LIFE

of a 4" difference from the garage floor level to the house's interior floor level. This is a safety requirement. The gases that may accumulate from exhausts or off gases of fuels are heavier than the air so they drop to the floor. It is also required that the floor have a slope to the exterior doors which allows the escape of these harmful gases. In most situations the level change requirement may be waived, but the floor must always maintain the required slope.

When a home is built on a basement, the level difference between the garage and the interior usually requires three steps, unless the foundation is modified as previously discussed. This level change makes it extremely difficult for someone in a wheelchair to use this entry. Many people with this special need build ramps inside the garage to access their home from this preferred and protected space. These ramps should follow Americans with Disabilities Act (ADA) requirements, which only permit a one inch rise for every twelve inches of run. An example would be: to travel up twenty-four inches (three eight inch steps), it requires twenty four feet of ramp. These ramps take over much of the garage space making this an impractical solution. Lifts are available but can be quite expensive; and usually inconvenient for the non-wheel user. Lowering the floor level of the interior of the house and raising the floor level of the garage will help even out the level change. Talk to your designer or builder before and during the excavation phase of your new house or modification and make sure the level change is as minor as possible.

The family entry is usually not as grand as the guest entry but its importance is greater. When designed properly, the family entry can truly enhance the quality of life for the those residing in the home. It can promote organization and create a welcoming experience when we arrive, and comforting and reassuring feelings when departing from our home.

FAMILY ENTRY SHOULD INCLUDE:
- Minor or no level changes
- Proximity to the kitchen
- A drop zone
- Coat, shoe, & boot storage
- A window seat or other seating
- Pantry
- Adjacency to bathroom
- A pleasant experience

CREATING HOUSES THAT WORK FOR LIFE

TRANSITIONAL ZONES

How we move from space to space and the adjacencies of these spaces effect how we dwell. One example of a transition space is the staircase. Typically the staircase of a two-story house lands in the front entry hall. The staircase is a wonderfully aesthetic design feature of a home and traditionally is showcased in the most public part of the house to make its impression on the visitor. When we follow the public vs. private, this location becomes questionable.

When we place the stairs in the front entry we also restrict the visual pleasure of the staircase from the family members who rarely enter or leave through the front door. It is possible to have the best of both worlds of a staircase. The landing of the staircase can be located in the private sector of the house with glimpses of the staircase visible from the front entry. This solution usually pleases everyone.

CREATING HOUSES THAT WORK FOR LIFE

One of my clients told me she thought I was out of my mind when I suggested that the staircase be placed away from the entry hall and rise from the corner of the great room adjacent to the parent's bedroom wing. After living in the home for a few months, she expressed how much they enjoyed this location. The staircase with its beautiful railings could be enjoyed from their family living area and the lower landing was located near the parent's bedroom and laundry making it convenient and comforting for the children.

Clients always have the last word and if they prefer a two-story space I will comply with a space that has detail and interest on all surfaces. The ceiling and upper walls are not to be forgotten, it is extremely important to apply architectural features to the ceiling and walls from the floor level up.

CREATING HOUSES THAT WORK FOR LIFE

Staircases are common in most houses. We use then to travel to the upper and lower floors of the house. It is standard for the staircase to be thirty-six inches wide. This width is too narrow and makes it difficult to move furniture, or pass someone going the other direction. Wider staircases at least 42" with deeper treads and shallower rises make it much easier for most to traverse up and down. A landing in the middle provides a safe resting place for those that may not be able to climb the full flight of steps all at one time. Many older residents have told me that as long as they have good hand rails and a resting place on the staircase, they can still climb up and down and appreciate the exercise.

Staircases leading to the lower level or basement are a huge threat to wheelchair users, especially those using power operated ones. A safety measure that works well is to change the direction of the staircase from the entry position. Most users can not manipulate the tight turn required to continue down the steps preventing a catastrophe from occurring.

The location of this staircase allows the family to appreciate its beauty from the main living space.

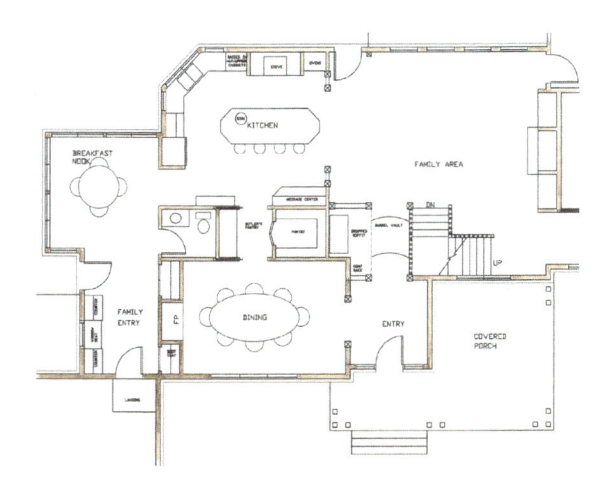

69

CREATING HOUSES THAT WORK FOR LIFE

This stair was designed for a family and their special needs child, the safe use of a motorized wheelchair was the goal for the orientation of the stair, the landing and change of direction. A gate across the opening of the stair may be used as another safety option. The elevator was relocated to achieve a circulation space inclusive for all.

When clients insist on a two-story house with all of the bedrooms on the second floor, I plan ahead and stack closets or spaces that would easily convert into an elevator shaft if needed. Renovating existing houses for some of these challenges can be quite expensive to resolve. It is always more cost effective to prepare for the "what ifs" during the initial construction of the home.

Some houses have the garage in the lower level making it can be quite difficult to obtain an accessible entry. I worked on a project that involved this type of situation. We were adding an addition on the back of the house. The existing house had a walkout basement with the garage entering the home at this lower level. The addition consisted of more living space on the main and lower levels. Since the clients were approaching their "golden years" and had every intention of staying in this home as long as it was possible, it was critical that it work for life. We all knew the need for an elevator was a good possibility but they weren't quite ready for it yet. In the addition, I placed a closet in the lower level which was adjacent to the entry from the garage and stacked another closet of the same dimension directly over it near the kitchen. Both will easily convert into the elevator shaft if the need arises.

CREATING HOUSES THAT WORK FOR LIFE

Hallways are another type of a transitional space. Many houses have the standard thirty-six inch wide hallway. This typical hallway is a long narrow passage usually to the bedroom wing of the house. The standard width is too narrow and poses many problems for the occupants of the house. Just passing another person can be difficult, not to mention moving furniture in and out of the adjacent spaces.

> *I experienced first hand a major problem with a narrow hallway. My mother was in her bedroom at the end of the hall, she was extremely ill and I had to call 911 for help. The paramedics could not get their equipment down the hallway and through the door because both were too narrow. She was conscience so they assisted her while she walked down the hallway to the gurney. She was very weak and this exertion intensified her illness. The paramedics expressed how common this problem is in most houses. Mom was able to walk with assistance but some patients are too ill and other provisions must be made. Sometimes collapsible gurneys are used but the tight corners are still difficult to maneuver without making it uncomfortable for the patient.*

The obvious solution of a narrow hallway is to widen it, but as designers we need to search even further for a better option. One approach would be to redesign the house to eliminate hallways all together. An enfilade scheme allows rooms to flow into each other without the use of hallways. This scheme doesn't make sense for transitioning into bedrooms, but the use of transitional nodes or interesting passageways are very effective. A transitional node is a circulation space. It should be a minimum of five feet square and may have openings to spaces in all directions. These nodes vary in shape and size but most are quite effective.

The hallway is too narrow for the passage of a gurney.

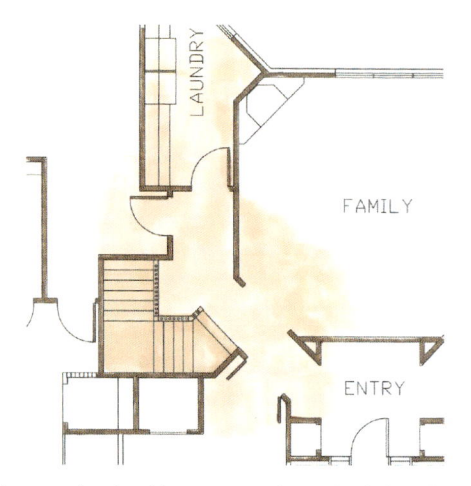

CREATING HOUSES THAT WORK FOR LIFE

A transition node should accommodate circulation in many directions, be an interesting space and large enough for accessibility and maneuverability.

Different styled doors offer solutions to many transitional problems. Pocket doors disappear into the wall making passage into another space the easiest. Some people have issues with pocket doors due to their poor performance in the past, but I have discovered when installed correctly the newer ones work great. Pocket doors offer an excellent option for tight passages and are perfect for bathrooms. Bi-fold doors and bi-pass doors are typically used on closets. Sliding doors, gliding doors, and French styled doors that swing into or out of the space, offer great options for transitions to the exterior as well as between interior rooms.

Door openings are also considered transitions. All door openings should be at least 32" wide, preferably 36". This width empowers the residents in many different ways. Wider doors make it easier to carry laundry baskets through, to move furniture in and out of rooms, to fit through with a child on your hip and one holding your hand; they allow assistance from another person, and last, but certainly not the least, wider doors are accessible for wheelchairs and wider people.

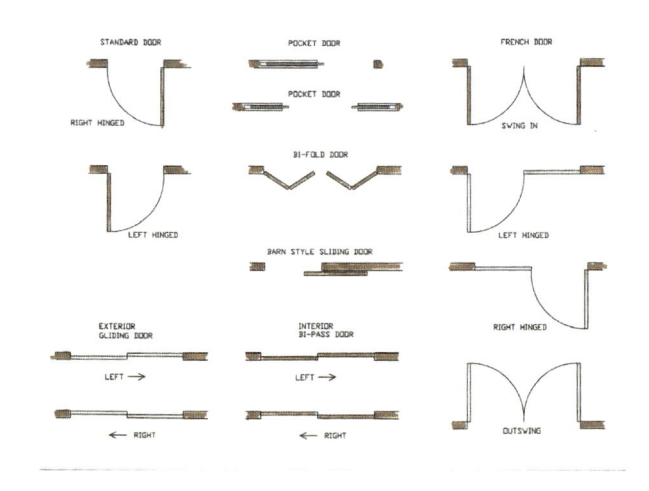

These are a few general door options.

CREATING HOUSES THAT WORK FOR LIFE

Transition areas can make or break how well a space works so consider your selections carefully. The hardware used to secure the door is critical to the success of how well it operates. Using levered styled door "knobs" makes life easier for everyone not just those suffering from a disability. They permit you to open a door with your elbow when carrying groceries, a child or laundry basket. Think of all the times you have had to sit something down to open the door because it required full use of your hand to turn the typical door knob. Levered hardware is now available in many finishes and styles to blend with your home's décor.

Transitional places are important and may offer design features that enhance the beauty of your home. They may include arched openings, passages flanked by columns, ceiling details, and floor material changes. An effective method to consider when rooms are directly connected is to form a portal by recessing the door a foot or so from the wall elevation. This creates a nice sense of transition which prevents the door from appearing to be a closet. In most houses transitions just occur out of the necessity of moving from one space to another, but when planned in a thoughtful way they can make your house work better and look great.

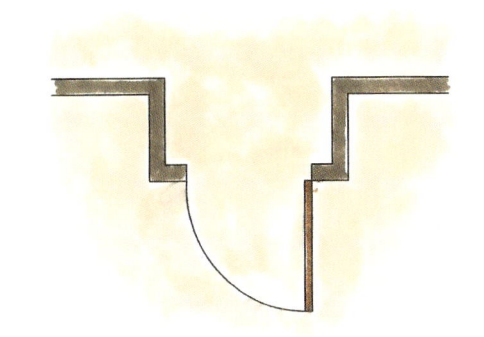

Recessing the door creates a portal or transition into the next room.

TRANSITION ZONES SHOULD INCLUDE:
- Staircases - minimum of 42" width, rise - no greater that 7", run – no less than 10",
- Staircases - at least one landing
- Staircases to lower level - Direction change at point of entry
- Staircases - Illumination
- Staircases - Hand and safety rails.
- 42" minimum passages, preferably 48"
- 32" minimum door openings, preferably 36"
- Doors with levered style hardware
- A sense of transition, portal to new space
- Provision for elevator
- Architectural detail
- Proper illumination

CREATING HOUSES THAT WORK FOR LIFE

THE KITCHEN

The kitchen is one of the most cherished spaces of the home. When a family entertains, it seems everyone always ends up in the kitchen. People love to hang out around an island, bar, or counter, maybe because of the food, but sometimes, it's just the place they want to be.

> *Before I renovated my home, the kitchen was very small. It was extremely difficult for anyone to share the space with me while preparing a meal or I was tripping all over them. I was amazed at how many times people still found their way into the small space and hung out before and after dinner. On many occasions I discovered my husband and his buddies hanging out, leaning against the counters, talking and laughing about life experiences. I kept all of this in mind while designing my new kitchen and provided ample room for lots of people to hang out in the kitchen without interfering in my work space.*

CREATING HOUSES THAT WORK FOR LIFE

Historically the kitchen or cooking space was removed from the house. Its heat and smells were considered offensive or uncomfortable for the residents and guests. It was also a fire hazard. Today it is the place where we prepare food, gather together as a family, and welcome our guests to share in all its activities. It has become the hearth of the home.

The kitchen may be considered the hearth of the home, but it also must serve as a work station. A kitchen that works considers all users and their individual needs for the space. A child can feel alienated in the kitchen with high counter tops and no place to see what's going on. Kids love to help in the kitchen, but there typically is no safe place for them to help or watch Mom as she prepares the meal. An elder person can share the same feelings. Most would love to help. They need to feel like they are still productive, but if they can't stand for lengthy periods, or climb onto a high bar stool, most kitchens can be quite challenging for them to manage. By offering multiple height work areas, we can include multiple users, and who wouldn't appreciate more help in the kitchen?

An extended counter may provide additional seated work space.

The days of the housewife have changed. Many members of the family may share the responsibility of food preparation. This requires more than one work station in the kitchen. Typical kitchens are designed with one working triangle. The triangle is the relationship of the refrigerator to the sink to the stove. For the kitchen to work for multiple users, we must look at different appliance and workstation relationships and offer several triangles. Center islands with a secondary sink, peninsulas and bar stools, movable carts, and counters that vary in height are some popular options.

CREATING HOUSES THAT WORK FOR LIFE

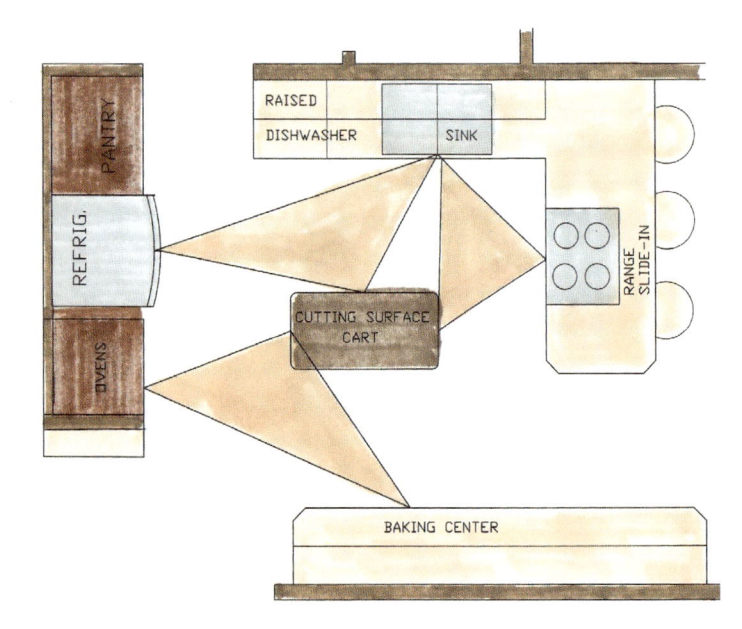

Multiple working triangles allow for more than one cook in the kitchen.

Passageways need to be wide enough for more than one user to work comfortably together in the kitchen. The standard thirty-six inch passage is too tight. I try to provide forty-eight inch passageways if possible but never less than forty-two.

Safety must always be a concern for all types of people using the kitchen. Rounded or chamfered corners on counter tops, soften the blow if one hits them with their hip, or for children - their head.

Appliances that are user friendly should always be considered. Cook-tops and ranges should have the controls located on the front edge so we are not required to reach across hot burners to change the settings. Microwave ovens should be placed at a height comfortable for all users. The microwave oven which is commonly placed over the range makes it impossible for children to use and is dangerous for everyone when the cook-top below is in use. Side by side refrigerators tend to be easier to access but many limit the size of the items to be stored. Newer refrigerator models offer wider openings in different door configurations.

The dishwasher is the most cherished appliance to most kitchen workers. However, if one has a lower back problem the dishwasher can cause some serious discomfort. Raising the dishwasher height can help alleviate some of the pain. Cabinet manufacturers are now offering dishwasher cabinets that range from seven to nine inches above the standard height. This change in height makes all the difference in the world to most users, but many are still reluctant to change. They just don't want to break

CREATING HOUSES THAT WORK FOR LIFE

the consistent counter top height to which we have become accustom. When convinced to raise the dishwasher, their response during the post occupancy evaluation is always positive. Until you experience the use of a raised dishwasher first hand, it is hard to comprehend how much difference these few inches make. Dishwasher drawers are another option. Some people prefer two drawers placed just under the counter; others stack them and raise the entire unit.

This application provides a higher surface and counter which conceals the view of the sink from the dinette.

Dishwasher drawers may be raised or placed directly under the counter. One or two drawers depend on family size and lifestyle. Some prefer two, one for clean dishes and one for dirty, which eliminates the need to ever unload to restock the cabinets.

This application at the end of the counter works well with the convenient dish rack for extra storage.

77

CREATING HOUSES THAT WORK FOR LIFE

Wall ovens are popular in today's kitchen and should be placed at a height comfortable and safe for the majority of users. The market now offers ovens that open like microwave ovens. Not having to reach over the drop down door makes it easier for all users, but especially for those with any type of disability.

Appliances are a major investment and should be researched carefully before purchased. They come in a variety of colors, finishes, styles and offer a range of options.

A moveable cart on lockable castors is an asset to any kitchen. Retailers are now marketing several styles and sizes for existing and new kitchens. A cart may be stored under a counter or island and pull out to provide a lower height work place. The surface can match the counter top or be made of wood to use as a cutting board, stainless steel, or marble which is great for rolling out pastry dough. Carts are a great option when the area of a kitchen is too small for a fixed island.

> *My kitchen is too narrow to accommodate an island and maintain the proper passage widths, so I use a cart in the center of the space. It works wonderfully as a cutting surface, serving counter, pastry board and other multiple uses. When preparing vegetables for a stir-fry I can unlock the casters and move the cart next to the stove for a convenient transfer to the skillet. Preparing the turkey for my large family gathering during the holiday is much easier since I have the cart. I can use the cart to transport the bird to and from the oven without having to carry it across the kitchen. This is a convenience for me now but later in my elder years it will most likely be a necessity.*

CREATING HOUSES THAT WORK FOR LIFE

The cart on casters is one of my favorite kitchen accessories. It is versatile, flexible and convenient.

Lighting is an important feature in all well designed spaces, but it is imperative to have proper lighting in the kitchen to insure the safety and cleanliness of our food. As we age the need for light increases. To make sure light levels work for life and for all users, kitchen illumination levels should meet the requirements of our elder population. The use of dimmers and zoning of fixtures to be operated by different switches allows for flexibility and light control.

Besides being a work place, the kitchen is also a place for entertaining. Today's kitchen must offer at least the same aesthetic appeal as the rest of the home. Lighting enhances the aesthetics and function of the space. General, task, ambient, under-counter, pendent style and natural light should all be considered in the design. The fixtures we choose should provide the light required for the task and be beautiful.

General light may be provided from many types of fixtures, but a popular treatment is the recessed or can light. These fixtures are installed flush with the ceiling surface and are usually spaced about four feet apart to effectively illuminate the room. Ambient light might be a series of puck lights, named because of their similarity to a hockey puck, illuminating a display case or wine rack. LED lights are now available in many configurations and used as accents throughout the home. Under-counter lights add to the ambience of the space but also add much needed counter light. If all illumination comes from the ceiling, the counter space directly

CREATING HOUSES THAT WORK FOR LIFE

under the wall cabinets is in shadow. Pendant and chandelier type fixtures, the jewelry of the space, not only provide illumination, but are attractive decorative pieces that enhance the beauty of any space.

My husband is an electrician and my kitchen is a perfect example of his work. Recessed lights, pendant lights, under-counter lights, accent lights and a chandelier over the table complete the effect and provide ample light for any task.

Fluorescent, incandescent, and low voltage fixtures are all popular in kitchen design. They each have advantages and disadvantages, so it is beneficial to understand the differences before making your selection.

CREATING HOUSES THAT WORK FOR LIFE

LIGHTING OPTIONS

Fluorescent illumination is more energy efficient but may offer a cooler color of light than incandescent. Some fluorescent bulbs require a few seconds to reach full capacity when first turned on. Fluorescents may be used as under-counter tube shaped lights, light bulbs in recessed fixtures, or bulbs in a decorative fixture.

Incandescent illumination provides a warm light, similar to sunlight and is at full capacity instantly. They have been popular for years, but new technology is quickly replacing their use due to their poor energy efficiency. Most fixtures will now work properly with either fluorescent or incandescent bulbs.

Low Voltage -Halogen fixtures come in a variety of shapes and sizes and are commonly used as under-counter or specialty lights. Puck lights are typically halogen fixtures. LED fixtures are becoming very popular and are available in many different styles and configurations. Used as under-counter lights and ambient light but do not provide enough foot-candles for general lighting.

Natural light and how it does or doesn't enter a room is often overlooked in residential design, but natural light provides a sense of warmth and comfort that artificial light can not achieve. Most kitchens are used during morning, noon, and night. Morning sunlight is wonderful to experience while eating breakfast, having a cup of coffee and reading the morning paper. Midday light warms the space and may nourish the spirit while we nourish our bodies with food. Enjoying a sunset during dinner would be a nice way to relax at the end of a busy day. Consider the location of the kitchen and which time of day you want natural light to enter and plan your layout accordingly.

Many cabinet companies offer a huge variety of amenities that enhance the cooking experience. Cabinets should offer storage that is easily accessible to all users. Base cabinets should have pull out storage and drawer space. Corner cabinets may be a Lazy-Susan type, but if recycling is desired, and it should be, garbage and recycling bins work great in the corner space.

CREATING HOUSES THAT WORK FOR LIFE

This lazy-Susan garbage and recycling bin makes recycling convenient for all.

Not having to get on your knees to retrieve pots and pans from a lower cabinet is easy for young cooks but imperative for those of us that may not be able to get back up.

Sink base cabinets now offer a working drawer at the bottom instead of a fake drawer front at the top of the cabinet. This lower drawer works great for towel storage makes the storage space under the sink easier to access, but may limit the open space under the sink. This might be a problem for plumbers installing a garbage disposal if they are not informed of this type of cabinet before the plumbing is roughed in. With a little customization this lower drawer can be made into a step that allows children to reach the sink independently. The sink is a tricky area when trying to apply an inclusive design philosophy. We strive to make our homes accessible, but to lose the storage space under the sink to allow for wheelchair accessibility does not make sense unless an occupant in the home is using a wheelchair. A second sink is becoming popular in kitchen design and can sometimes help solve some accessibility issues.

CREATING HOUSES THAT WORK FOR LIFE

Upper wall cabinets should offer visible storage as well as closed storage. Open shelves and cabinets with glass fronts adds a nice dimension to the kitchen, but they also help a person with Dementia or Alzheimer find their food. I prefer wall cabinets to go all the way to the ceiling, without a dropped ceiling or open storage above. The dropped ceiling is a waste of space and the open area is a great look but can be very difficult to maintain. Kitchens get dirty easily from cooking residue, the open shelve above the cabinets is no exception to this, as dirt and grime collect on the items displayed and on the top of the cabinet. Reaching this space for cleaning is dangerous. It requires a ladder or step stool placed precariously because the lower cabinet protrudes further than the upper ones do. Cabinets that extend all the way to the ceiling can be difficult for the majority of users to access but if seldom used items are placed on the upper shelves they stay clean in the enclosed space.

The use of this drawer adds much needed space for towel storage.

Glass doors and open storage provide space to display dishes and accessories. Cabinets that extend to the ceiling look great and are much easier to clean than those with an open space above.

CREATING HOUSES THAT WORK FOR LIFE

The cabinets are a standard 24" deep but this refrigerator is 36". A recess in the wall was designed to receive the addition depth of the refrigerator to maintain line of cabinets and not protrude into room.

It is common for standard refrigerators to protrude out from the base cabinets several inches. Base cabinets are twenty-four inches deep and most refrigerators are deeper. There are several brands available that offer a twenty-four inch deep refrigerators, but they are usually pretty pricey. I prefer to place the refrigerator in a location that permits it to be even with the base cabinets by recessing the wall to receive the additional dimension. I also place a pantry cabinet, wall oven cabinet or other twenty-four inch deep full height cabinet next to the refrigerator. Instead of the standard twelve inch deep wall cabinet that is typically above the refrigerator, I use a twenty-four inch cabinet. This creates an even wall unit and provides clean storage for the stuff that usually ends up on top of the refrigerator.

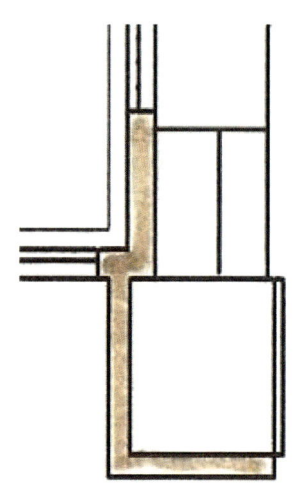

The depth should be determined by the size of refrigerator however 36" is usually adequate.

CREATING HOUSES THAT WORK FOR LIFE

Cabinet hardware (handles) and faucets should be easy for all users to operate, including those with arthritic hands. Pull knobs tend to be difficult to grasp, but handles wide enough for fingers to slide under work well. Levered faucet controls work better than rounded, hard to grasp knobs, and a high arching faucet allows more clearance for large pots and pans to be washed. A retractable spray nozzle makes it easier to fill large vessels with water while resting on the counter top.

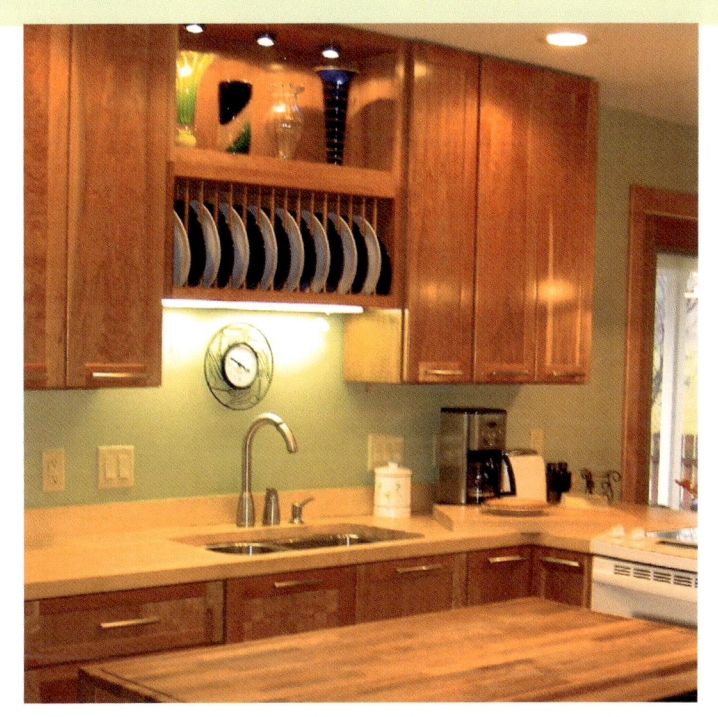

Wide handles, levered faucet with retractable spray nozzle and high arch offer convenience and ease for all users.

Solid surface and granite countertops are very popular but do not fit in everyone's budget. Laminate surfaces still offer an affordable option and can be fabricated with a contrasting edge which helps aging eyes depict a difference from the counter top to the floor. Counter selections should be made very carefully. I have discovered that most consumers do not research enough about the products they choose and are often disappointed with the results. Granite comes in a range of colors and finishes. Black shiny surfaces show smears and finger prints and require a lot of attention. Most solid surface products require regular maintenance. They need to be treated with conditioners periodically to maintain the desired look and performance. There are many resources available to help you find out as much as you can before selecting your countertop material. Countertops are usually a substantial investment and not easily changed.

CREATING HOUSES THAT WORK FOR LIFE

The family message center works great near or within the kitchen area. This space may include a place for the telephone, cook book storage, note pads, chalk board, bulletin board, desk, file drawers, family computer, and a mail sorting area. Today's households require more and more equipment to function properly, so it is best to consider all needs during the planning stage.

The message center provides an alternative height surface, storage for the gourmet's library and is necessary for organization of household messages.

Kitchens are probably the most difficult space to design for all users. The guidelines discussed above are intended to make every user's life a little easier, but if a resident requires the long-term use of a wheelchair other accommodations might need to be implemented. These special accommodations compromise the functional aspects for those not in a wheelchair and should not be considered unless long-term wheelchair use is required. Toe kick space under base cabinet can be raised from the standard dimension of four inches to nine which permits a closer approach and reduces the damage that often occurs from the wheelchair. The sink base, cook top and a section of work space should be lowered and open underneath to provide access for the seated user. Counter heights might need to be lowered and all storage should be within reach.

CREATING HOUSES THAT WORK FOR LIFE

I collaborated on a project with a person requiring a wheelchair and was amazed at the technological advancements in wheelchair design. Her motorized wheelchair enabled her to move about in most spaces, it lifted permitting her to reach heights that I can't even reach. I questioned her about her personal kitchen's design and realized that few if any special accommodations had been needed because of the technological features of her wheelchair. These wheelchairs are extremely expensive and not all users are able to afford them, but hopefully the advancements will continue and become more affordable for all of those in need.

My specialty is space design but product designers are challenged by the same consumers' needs. Design is so much more than the creation of beauty it is the solution to many of life's problems.

"Design is so much more than the creation of beauty; it is the solution to many of life's problems."

THE KITCHEN SHOULD INCLUDE:
- Multiple height work stations
- Minimum of 2 working triangles
- Minimum of 48" wide passages
- Rounded or chamfered corners on counters
- Raised dishwasher or dish washing drawers
- Micro wave & wall oven at comfortable heights for all users
- Seated work stations
- Appropriate hardware and faucets for arthritic hands
- General overhead lighting, under cabinet lighting, ambient lighting
- Cart on casters
- Accessible pullout storage
- Hidden and visible storage
- Easily maintained materials
- Contrast between surfaces
- Family message center

CREATING HOUSES THAT WORK FOR LIFE

PERSONAL CARE AREAS

The bathroom has become one of the most luxurious places in the home. But even with all of the finest materials and amenities, the bathroom can still be a very dangerous place for many people. Most home accidents occur in the bathroom. It is common, for little or no attention to be given to this fact when designing the space. We must fully understand all of the tasks that need to be performed and the different types of users, to create bathrooms that are safe, luxurious and empowering.

This bathroom is safe, versatile and luxurious.

Bathrooms have advanced greatly throughout history. They have gone from the outhouse to the inside and become a place of convenience and luxury. The use of expensive materials, elaborate fixtures and huge amounts of space have become a common request from many clients. The show-homes of today have set the precedence for the expectations of the average homeowner. They want the spa tubs, elaborate showers, double bowled vanities and secluded toilet rooms. What many don't realize is these popular bathrooms, with all of their amenities, do little to ensure our safety.

CREATING HOUSES THAT WORK FOR LIFE

It is common for master suites in average priced newer home's to include:
- A spa tub awkwardly placed in the room with at least one step resulting in sharp corners and no opportunity for grab bars.
- Seat-less small showers with curbed entries, no grab bars and narrow doors.
- A double bowled vanity at the typical thirty-two inch height which is uncomfortable for most of us.
- A secluded, inaccessible toilet.

The majority of bathrooms in older homes, and those in newer houses that aren't the in the master's suite, are a typical 5' x 7' dimension. The size was dictated by the standard bathtub, a toilet and a small vanity. This narrow width doesn't allow enough space for accessibility or for assistance. The doors typically enter into the space posing a serious threat to any person that falls down or becomes ill and collapses on the floor. The usable floor space of the bathroom is also the space required for the door to swing open. If one's body is occupying that space, the paramedics cannot get to them without taking the door off the hinges. This wastes valuable time in a medical emergency.

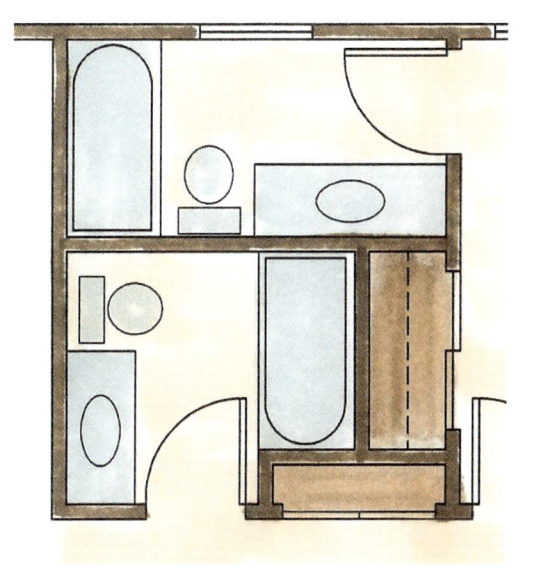

These doors open into the floor space of the bathroom, making it necessary for paramedics to remove the door from its hinges if someone collapses in the floor and requires medical attention.

"A bathroom that works for life begins with an entry door that does not swing into a space designated for any other use in the bathroom."

CREATING HOUSES THAT WORK FOR LIFE

A bathroom that works for life begins with an entry door that does not swing into a space designated for any other use in the bathroom. This access may be achieved with the use of a pocket door. Pocket doors disappear into the wall, allowing a clear entry for all users. They require no door jamb, so when space is minimal this style of door solves many problems. Pocket doors do require wall space for the door to recede. This can be a design challenge in a new house, but it is sometimes impossible to achieve in an existing house renovation. Standard pocket door hardware is not the best. There are newer, easier to operate options. You might have do some research to find them, but they are available.

Doors that swing out from the bathroom would also permit access in the case of an emergency, but bathrooms usually enter from a hallway or other transition space which poses the problem of hitting someone as they pass by.

A house should have at least one bath tub, preferably located in the children's area of the home. We bathe young children, we do not shower them. Regardless of where a tub is located, or how luxurious, it should still be as safe as possible. Tub areas should have skid or slip resistant surfaces with grab bars for a safe transition in and out. Grab bars are a must for safety, they can be decorative and substitute as towel bars, but a towel bar can never substitute as a grab bar. Grab bars must be installed according to manufacturer's recommendations. If a homeowner chooses not to install grab bars at the time of construction, blocking should still be provided in the wall for future installation.

Showers tend to be the most popular option for personal hygiene. There are many shower units on the market, but few offer an accessible entry. Custom showers are rarely accessible either, but should be. Curbs are common on even the most elaborate shower rooms. Many believe a curb is necessary to retain the water, but I can assure you they are not in the majority of applications. The curb creates more problems than it solves. We tend to stub our toes on them, have difficulty or the inability to lift our leg over them and we definitely cannot roll a walker or wheelchair across them.

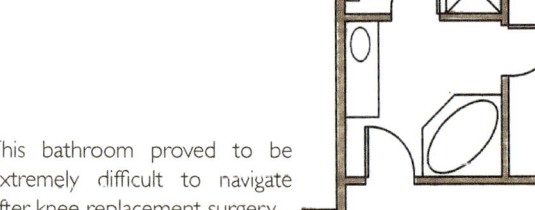

This bathroom proved to be extremely difficult to navigate after knee replacement surgery.

CREATING HOUSES THAT WORK FOR LIFE

I have a very dear friend in her fifties that required knee replacement surgery. This medical necessity has become extremely popular in our society. She had recently built a new "cookie cutter home", and even though I preached to her to make the needed changes, she felt she just couldn't afford them. She returned home after the surgery and soon realized how difficult her house was to maneuver. Upon her return home from the hospital she was faced with three steps up to the entry door and no hand rail for assistance. Her shower stall is a 3' x 3' standard unit. It has a curb, no grab bars and no seat. She struggled to lift her leg over the curb into the shower. With nothing to hold for security, or to help support the weight on her other knee, her first shower was "scary". She can no longer use the spa tub in the corner of her bathroom. The style and lack of grab bars for support require her to get on her knees to lift herself out of the tub. Once you have had knee replacement surgery you are not permitted to kneel.

This bathroom was built in a condominium complex intended for retirement age residents. The shower is extremely small and has a curbed entry, the toilet is very low and provides no opportunity for a grab bar, and the space is very tight and could never be accessible. "Typical bathroom design."

A curb-less or step-free entry that is wide enough for a wheelchair provides a pleasant experience for all of us. The shower base is formed to slope toward the drain allowing the water to flow away from the door opening. A glass shower door, with a gasket at the bottom to prevent water leakage, extends to the floor level. This is effective and a nice look. The only time a curb-less entry might not work is when multiple shower heads are used with a standard drainage system. Spa showers are the latest trend in luxury baths. The water supply from multiple heads is too great for a standard drain to handle, causing water to pool before going down the drain. This is not a good idea for

CREATING HOUSES THAT WORK FOR LIFE

a curb-less shower or even a shower with a curb. The drain in this application should be engineered by a professional to make sure it can handle the amount of water that is supplied.

This shower is beautiful and it works! It has a curb-less entry, grab bar, hand held adjustable shower head, levered faucet, seat, slip resistant floor and patterned glass door that requires less cleaning.

Inside the shower stall we should find: grab bars, a seat, shampoo and soap storage, and appropriate faucets. Grab bars in the shower are critical to everyone's safety and should always be installed. The misconception of grab bars compromising the look is common, but they are now quite attractive. They help us balance while washing the bottom of our feet and help us rise from the seated position. They provide a secure place for us to grab quickly if we happen to lose our balance. Seats in the shower are extremely beneficial. Due to weakness or pain, it is usually impossible to stand for the duration of a shower shortly after a major surgery or illness, but nothing feels better than that first shower. The seat should be large enough for all users, a minimum of fifteen inches deep and thirty inches wide. Seats and grab bars provide the elder user a safe place to let the therapeutic water flow over their body. They also provide a comfortable place for women to safely shave their legs. Shower faucets come in a variety of designs. The most effective are the handheld showerheads that mount onto a slide bar. These offer versatility for many types of users, tall, short and seated. Levered control handles are easily operated by all, but essential for arthritic hands. A scald proof device is a good idea and required by most code regulations. Soap and shampoo storage works best when built as a niche or recess into the wall.

CREATING HOUSES THAT WORK FOR LIFE

This eliminates any protrusion into the space that could be a safety concern. Storage space for the necessities in a shower eliminates them from being placed on the seat. The storage space and water controls should be easily accessed from the seated position.

Flooring and wall surfaces in a shower should be easy to maintain. Flooring must be slip resistant. Tiled showers are beautiful, but grout can be difficult to clean and maintain. Grout needs to be sealed frequently due to its porosity. Material selections for a shower should be carefully considered. There are many products on the market to explore. Do your research so you're not disappointed later.

One of my favorite materials to use is a cultured marble product. It functions well on the floors and wall surfaces, looks good and is very easy to clean and maintain. Custom shower stalls are not cheap, they are a major investment, but when designed and installed well, they are worth the cost.

Different size users require different height vanities. If you are at least 5'6" you probably realize that brushing your teeth can be very uncomfortable at a standard height vanity. Offering two different heights and two sinks is a good idea in an owner's suite.

If only one sink is possible, try a 36" height in the owner's suite and a standard height, (32"), in the children's bathroom.

Varied height vanities, French style doors, levered faucets in a contemporary style offer another option for a bathroom to work.

The location and height of the toilet can also effect how well, or not, the space works. Toilet rooms have become popular in new homes. I am not a fan of these spaces because they usually are not accessible and I find them rather unpleasant to occupy. Even in the most luxurious bathrooms, toilet rooms can be extremely small and have narrow doors that even a moderately heavy person would have difficulty passing through.

CREATING HOUSES THAT WORK FOR LIFE

I have seen toilet room doors that swing into the space, hit the toilet, and require one to straddle the toilet to close the door.

Some clients still insist on a toilet room. These spaces should be accessible, or at least easily converted. Toilets come in three sizes: standard (lowest height), comfort (middle height), and accessible (highest height). I usually place an accessible height toilet in the owner's suite, a comfort height toilet is perfect in a powder room or half-bath and a standard height toilet works best in the children's bathroom. Until toilet technology advances and affordable toilets automatically adjust to fit the user, this seems to be the best solution.

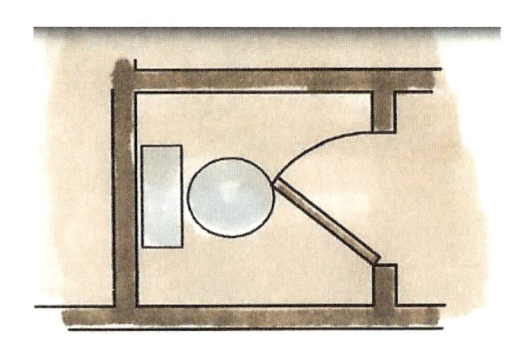

It is way too common for toilet room spaces to function like this one. I have personally experienced these spaces and reviewed drawings like this one; I just don't understand how anyone could think this was ok.

The general size of the bathroom may vary, but a 5' turnaround is required for accessibility. This dimension also works well if assistance is needed and presents itself as a comfortable well proportioned room.

Bathrooms are extremely important areas when evaluating how well a house functions. Most home accidents happen in the bathroom, so safety is a huge issue. As we age, become ill or injured, the safety, security and empowerment offered by the bathroom may dramatically affect our lives. Many people would prefer to age or recover in their own home, but when the bathroom is not safe or does not allow for the needed services, most are forced to age or recover in a healthcare facility.

CREATING HOUSES THAT WORK FOR LIFE

PERSONAL CARE AREAS SHOULD INCLUDE:

- 5' clear floor space
- 36" minimum door – pocket door or door swing with separate entry space
- An easily maintained and slip resistant flooring surface
- Bathtub in at least one bathing area with grab bars, skid resistant surfaces and no step entry
- No protruding corners, especially around the tub area
- Shower with 36" wide curb-less or roll-in entry, 48"X 48" clear space, seat, grab bars, adjustable hand held shower head, levered scald proof controls, soap and shampoo storage accessible from the seated position, and skid resistant flooring
- Varied heights vanities
- Appropriate task lighting and ambient lighting
- Toilet room accessibility – 36" minimum swing out or pocket door if any
- Toilet height options – standard, comfort, accessible
- Storage – linens and medicine
- Adjacency to dressing and bedroom areas

LAUNDRY CARE AREAS

Laundry facilities can make a big difference in the overall function of a home. The laundry care station can be tucked within a deep closet or within a large room used for several different functions. Commonly its location has varied from the basement, near or as a part of the family entry, off the kitchen, or near the owner's suite. It has traditionally been considered a secondary space with little importance to the average resident, except for the person who does the laundry.

CREATING HOUSES THAT WORK FOR LIFE

After living in her home for a month, one of my clients referred to the laundry room as "command central". This comment said a lot about the success of the design for this space and where we had placed it within the layout of the floor plan. We located it next to the owner's suite near the landing of the staircase that led up to the children's bedrooms. This location makes much more sense than the typical placement in the basement or near the family entry of the home.

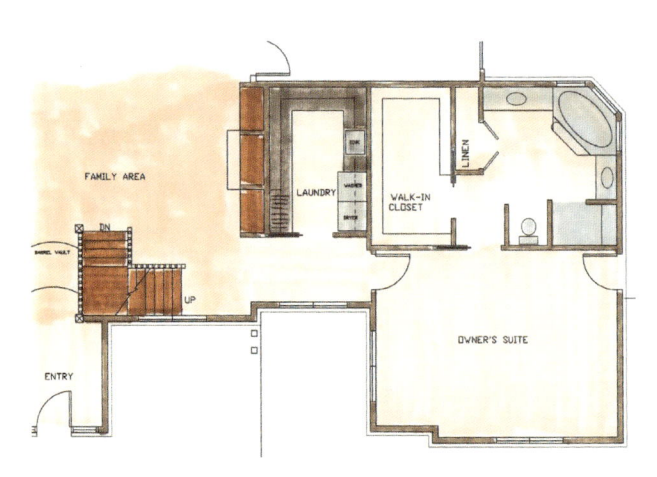

"Command Central"

Historically the laundry was adjacent to the kitchen because of plumbing requirements and the kitchen was where the homemaker spent most of her time during the day. This adjacency made some sense then, but it still required the laundress to gather the soiled clothes from the bedroom areas, carry them to the laundry room (which was usually located at the opposite end of the home), then back again after washing the clothes. Many current houses still follow this same planning scheme; however, most contemporary women are not in the kitchen any longer, they are out of the home working at their other job.

A laundry that really works not only provides a functional layout with appropriate appliances to complete the tasks of washing and caring for clothing and linens, but is placed within the home in the most convenient place for all users. Laundry rooms located near the bedrooms, where our clothes are stored, is a better solution. When bedroom areas are divided, children in one location and parents in another, try to keep the laundry near the owner's suite who will continue to reside in the home after the children have moved.

Laundry rooms can be noisy. The noise produced by washing machines and dryers needs to be addressed especially when a common wall is shared between the laundry and bedroom. I have found that many people will do a load or two of clothes in the evening which might cause a problem for an early to bed partner.

Laundry rooms have become fairly complex with a variety of equipment and requirements. Laundry areas need a lot of storage. Many clients request a drying rack for clothing that needs to lie flat, a hanging rack for drip-drying, or for freshly laundered clothes to be placed when just out of the dryer. They always want a folding place. Home dry cleaning equipment is now available and requires special attention; it can be large and require additional space and electrical outlets.

I prefer to conceal the soiled clothes within a storage closet or cabinet, but open storage shelves can be attractive when decorative baskets are used. Shelving or cabinets to store household cleaning supplies and laundry supplies should be easily reached. Storage above the appliances is acceptable for taller users but a lower alternative space should also be provided.

Hanging racks for dry clothes can be placed easily, but drip-dry racks might require a basin with a drain. In order for clothes to dry flat a fairly large surface is needed. Netting that stretches over another surface, or large shelving stacked that pulls out from the wall, are alternatives. The folding place could be a counter top, table top or cart with drop leaf sides.

Tall pantry cabinets serve well to keep dirty laundry sorted and out of sight. Upper cabinets were installed at a height to accommodate future front load machines.

A deep sink within a counter works well for the majority, but varied height requirements and accessibility issues could arise. A free standing accessible sink might be a better option. The sink area may be used for many other functions than for laundry. Some people are avid gardeners and like a work place for potting and propagating household plants. Crafts and artwork are popular and often require a seated work area as well as a sink.

CREATING HOUSES THAT WORK FOR LIFE

This space was the kitchen when I moved into the house, when we converted it to the laundry we maintained the sink and counter.

Raising front load machines and placing them under a higher counter or wall cabinets makes the appliances easier to access, but tend to make the upper counter and/or cabinets difficult to reach. A lower table or counter with storage space should also be available as an alternative.

Ironing board and iron storage are essential for most laundry rooms. The ironing board may be free standing or housed within a special wall cabinet. Wall cabinet ironing boards are usually fixed and do not offer any flexibility for different user heights or locations.

Designing all work areas of the home requires a lot of information about the residents and how they intend to use the space. It is extremely important to listen and understand the way they wish to function within these spaces, but it is also the designer's responsibility to inform the user if there are more effective and efficient ways to achieve their goals. We are creatures of habit, but some habits need to be broken.

LAUNDRY CARE STATIONS SHOULD INCLUDE:

- Raised front load appliances
- Counter space / folding area / flat clothes drying space
- Greater than a 5' clearance
- Soiled clothes storage
- Sink and hanging rack
- Ironing board storage
- Laundry supplies and cleaning supplies storage
- Sewing center / seated work space
- Adjacency to dressing areas

CREATING HOUSES THAT WORK FOR LIFE

SLEEPING QUARTERS

Bedrooms and bathrooms are the most intimate and private areas in the home. These places should be located in the most private area of the house. Often in newer homes, the owner's suite is adjacent to the foyer with little or no transition into the space. This location breaks the rules of a public to private concept.

The activities that commonly occur in the bedroom have expanded in modern day living. The square footage requirements have increased as well. The bedroom used to have a bed, dresser, chest of drawers and maybe a chair. The spaces were small and regarded as secondary. Today the owner's suite is expected to be as grand as the main living spaces of the home. It is required to offer a place to sleep, lounge, watch TV, exercise, read a book and have a cup of tea, to name a few. Even in the most modest home; a walk-in closet the size of a small bedroom adjacent to a fully equipped bathing facility, are now standard.

Some newer two-story houses provide an owner's suite on the first floor; few even offer a suite on each level. This is one solution to the problem that occurs when parents have young children and want to be on the same level, but when children are older they prefer the separation different levels can provide. Having two suites also provides the opportunity for multi-generational residents; Grandma and Grandpa residing with the younger residents, but typically two suites are just not within the budget.

CREATING HOUSES THAT WORK FOR LIFE

Some homeowners still prefer all bedrooms to be located on the second floor. This tends to hurt the salability of the home and is in direct conflict with trans-generational and inclusive design philosophies. When clients insist that all bedrooms be upstairs, I provide a stacked storage space that may be easily converted to a future elevator or lift if needed. Another option is to have a home office or other space on the first floor that could also be used as a first floor bedroom and bath.

Children's bedrooms are important spaces. They need a place to call their own, a place to personalize and a place for privacy, even if shared with a sibling. Some larger homes provide a bedroom and bathroom for each child, but in most situations, whether they share a bedroom or not, it is still common for children to share a bathroom.

Bedrooms are a great place for custom furniture and built-ins. Window seats offer storage and can be a great place for many different activities; children might curl up and read a book, play with toys or sit and visit a friend. Sounds idealistic, doesn't it? They most likely will be texting someone or talking on their cell phone. Built-in desks and bookcases add a level of detail and dimension to, what is too often, a boring space.

This bedroom is tight so I designed custom built-in storage. The three lower drawers pivot open, the center opens to reveal shelves for bedside accessories, and the top three sections are doors concealing three large shelves for sweaters and casual ware. The interior edge curves to permit operation as well as providing a smooth rounded surface instead of a sharp edge at bedside.

Bedrooms need to be a place for expression and personalization. They should be flexible so they may change as the child matures. Bedroom furniture comes in many different styles and dimensions. Some is designed to modify as the child grows and their needs change. Themed designs have become quite popular in children's areas from the nursery to the teenager's room, but are often expensive applications and not frequently changed. Built-in furnishings sound permanent, but when designed

CREATING HOUSES THAT WORK FOR LIFE

with flexibility they may easily be modified to adapt to changing personal desires.

Personalization of space is inherent to comfort. A place that reflects the person that resides within it offers security and comfort to that person. This is extremely important in bedroom spaces.

> SLEEPING QUARTERS SHOULD PROVIDE:
> - Ample space for furniture and circulation
> - Appropriate furniture for occupants needs
> - Large accessible closet – 36" door minimum
> - Built-in storage, desk, window seat
> - Flexibility
> - Adjacency to personal care area
> - Personalization opportunities

BUSINESS/COMPUTER ROOMS

Home office spaces require planning. Many people are working in some aspect from their home, others prefer a designated space to conduct the business of the running a household. Home businesses were traditionally conducted from a spare bedroom, but in newer houses an office space adjacent to the front entry is common. When in view of the entry, offices are furnished with desk and chair, built-in cabinetry and guest chairs. This can be a quite handsome space, but might not function properly for the most effective worker.

When deciding on a location or designing the space, we should consider the equipment needed for the home based business. Lighting requirements, file storage, reference library, computer, phone, facsimile, printer, storage, chairs, work surface and how many people will be using the space all come into play. Ergonomically designed work

CREATING HOUSES THAT WORK FOR LIFE

stations are usually much more effective than most formal looking office furniture. Professional office designers and office system planners spend hours researching and documenting how a space needs to be used. In residential offices this important step is often left out.

The home office space should be planned to easily convert to another usage such as a bedroom or mother-in-law quarters. Home offices are great when they are needed, but can end up as a wasted space when the need is no longer there.

Home Offices Should Include:
- Separate entry or adjacency to public entry if business type requires visitors
- Should be easily converted into another type space
- Ergonomic layout and furniture
- Research of requirements

EATING PLACES

Most modern day homes offer many places to eat; formal dining room, kitchen table, breakfast nook, island or bar, covered porch, patio, deck, sunroom, bedroom, or maybe just the coffee table. Different lifestyles require a variety of places for eating. Even in our modern day rushed lives, with more and more meals eaten out, dining at home is still very important to most people. We need places to eat when entertaining large groups, small gatherings, intimately and alone.

Natural and artificial light is essential to all spaces, but can really affect our eating places. Lighting plays a huge role in the ambience of a place. It can set the mood for whatever type of eating you prefer. Breakfast nooks should have east exposure to natural light. The morning sun will brighten anyone's day. Formal dining rooms are typically used in the evening, so west exposure can cause a

CREATING HOUSES THAT WORK FOR LIFE

problem if window treatments are not effective in controlling the sunlight.

The room should be illuminated in a variety of methods. The right decorative light fixture over a dining table can make a big difference in the look and feel of the room. Illumination around the perimeter of the ceiling is a subtle effect that enhances the ambience of the space. Spot lights will accentuate paintings or millwork. In the selection of fixtures we should consider the color of light, direction of light and amount of light provided. A chandelier might incorporate up light, down light and be controlled by switches to allow different options.

Bar stools are a great option, but may not work for everyone.

The furniture we select for eating places should offer a variety of options and be scaled to fit comfortably witnn the space. Dining tables cannot be so large that the circulation of the space is compromised. A minimum 3' clearance around the table is preferred. People should be able to get up from the table and comfortably pass by other diners. Chairs and bar stools should be sturdy and stable. Higher bar stools and chairs are difficult for young and old alike to sit upon. A lower counter may be appropriate for youngsters, but can be uncomfortable for the very tall. Some people require chairs with arms to assist them in rising, others might feel too confined.

Eating places occur outside of the designated eating areas of the home too; like at the coffee table or curled up in a lounge chair in the corner of the family room. It is important to realize this when selecting and arranging these furniture pieces. To live comfortably in a house is to be worry free. If we are constantly concerned about a drink damaging the surface of a side table or the coffee table we can't enjoy life as we should. Relax, either select finishes that are durable and water resistant or keep coasters readily available to protect the surface. Proper placement of side tables, coffee tables, shelves or sturdy ottomans permits one to always have a surface available for the placement of refreshments.

CREATING HOUSES THAT WORK FOR LIFE

Storage in dining areas may be beautiful and functional.

Formal dining rooms are showcase rooms. They are located near the front entry to make an impression, but they must also be conveniently located near the kitchen. It works well to have a butler's pantry connect the two spaces. This space provides extra storage for china and formal glassware; it may offer a sink or serve as a bar. If a butler's pantry is too extravagant for the budget, built-in cabinetry is another option.

Eat-in kitchens provide a less formal approach to dining. They might incorporate a counter, bar or island with or without a table. Breakfast nooks can be fascinating spaces. They can be an open space for a table and chairs or a booth with table and built-in benches. They may be surrounded by

The butler's pantry is making a come back, they are convenient and provide a buffer between formal dining and the kitchen.

windows or tucked in a quiet corner.

As cool as built-in booths are, they can cause some difficulties. The act of scooting across the bench in a confined space can be hard for a person with even minor health issues. Being on the inside of a booth seat and needing to leave the space can be an inconvenience for others. A solution would be to build in one side and leave the other exposed so chairs may also be used. You can still have the experience and look desired combined with the flexibility of another seating option.

East facing eating place.

CREATING HOUSES THAT WORK FOR LIFE

Many of us prefer to dine outdoors, the same rules apply; appropriate and versatile furniture, artificial light and natural light control, a variety of surfaces and storage.

Eating is a social activity as well as a basic necessity. It has become so much more in our lives than just an activity to sustain one's body, it sustains one's life. Sharing a meal with family or friends should be relished, a time to relax and separate ourselves from the hustle and bustle of our daily activities. When dining we nurture our bodies and souls. Even when alone, the act of eating should be comforting.

Eating Places Should Provide:
- Adjacency to cooking area
- 36" minimum clearance around table
- Partially free standing – built-in booths and banquets are difficult to manage
- Bars and counter spaces should offer alternative height seating
- Varied levels of lighting for different effects
- Natural light, light control and views to the outside

CARE FREE LIVING

The family, living or great room are spaces within a home for the family. We may entertain guests there, curl up in a lounge chair and read a good book, gather to watch a favorite show on television, or have an intimate conversation.

Many of these spaces are huge rooms with towering ceilings and elaborate decoration. Upon first impression these spaces may seem quite grand and desirable. But for most, it is impossible to feel cozy and comfortable sitting in such a large space with sounds echoing off the tall ceilings.

CREATING HOUSES THAT WORK FOR LIFE

Lower ceilings and more intimate places relate better to the human scale. We can still have more square footage and higher than standard ceilings, but within reason. The openness of a great room and the functional qualities it offers is preferred by most homeowners. It is a flexible space; it allows us to be together as families during quiet evenings, or to entertain friends, at large gatherings. The host or hostess feels as much a part of the event as the guests do. Great rooms allow Mom to keep a watchful eye on playful children while preparing dinner or to observe and assist the studious student while doing their homework.

The open layout may also pose some problems if not carefully planned. Spaces can feel too open if no sense of separation is provided. Sounds from one activity may disturb another. Open plans work best when they provide intimate spaces within. The warmth of a fireplace with built-in bookcases, a hearth, and side chairs evoke a sense of seclusion and comfort for many.

Rooms can be adjacent and still provide the same experience as the openness of the great room. A kitchen and dinette might have a visual separation without any physical barrier. The family can be next to the kitchen and separated by only a circulation core, counter or bar.

Living areas can be of many shapes and sizes. They should be flexible to accommodate the many different activities that may take place within them.

Spaces can be visible and function as a whole but still maintain independence from one another. This is the view from the family area into the kitchen.

CREATING HOUSES THAT WORK FOR LIFE

ENTERTAINMENT AREAS

Entertainment areas may include game tables, bars, large screen TVs, exercise equipment, electronic games, etc. They may be a designated space or take place in any living area. An understanding of the equipment and operational requirements and furniture is imperative to the proper design of these spaces.

Entertainment areas should be designed for both family and guests. Questions to be answered are: How many users, what are the needs of those users and what activities will take place? Some families require a bar area, some want a game table. Other families will require both and must have space for a billiard table or exercise equipment.

Programming a space is much easier when designing for a specific family's needs, but when designing a market house or for future usages this space can be quite challenging.

Lower level (basement), requirements tend to vary from those on a main floor. Kitchenettes, theatre rooms and exercise rooms are popular in basement entertainment areas; while wet bars and hearth rooms are common on the main floor.

This basement offers a second kitchen, hearth area and pool table for entertaining.

Entertainment areas in the lower level are typically inaccessible. For these spaces to work for everyone, a lift or an accessible entry in a walk-out situation should be considered.

Creating spaces that provide ample room for changing or multiple functions, and still feel comfortable, can be achieved with creative furniture placement and space differentiation. Furniture can define a space when arranged properly and grounded with an area rug. A large open space may be visually divided by floor material changes and/or ceiling details. Most

CREATING HOUSES THAT WORK FOR LIFE

structural columns cannot be moved. When we incorporate these columns into the design they disappear or look as though they are supposed to be there.

CONVERSATION AREAS

Conversation takes place throughout the home but we can intentionally create areas to sit down and talk. Most rooms have a multitude of activities that take place within them and all activities need to be addressed in planning. Noise from other activities may distract from an intimate conversation. Provide quiet, out of the way places with comfortable furniture arranged in a manner to promote conversation. Seating areas for a variety of user types, and types of use, are important throughout the home. Some gatherings are for two, some for larger groups. User types would include children, young adults, adults and the elders. These users come in all shapes and sizes. Some furniture is not appropriate for some people. Children need furniture scaled to them and elder users can find it difficult to get up and down from many styles of sofas and chairs. Some gatherings require a more formal setting while others would find a large throw pillow on the floor quite comfortable.

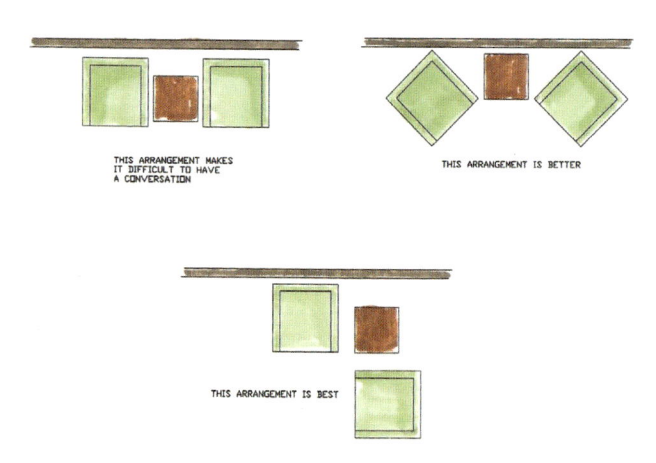

THIS ARRANGEMENT MAKES IT DIFFICULT TO HAVE A CONVERSATION

THIS ARRANGEMENT IS BETTER

THIS ARRANGEMENT IS BEST

LOUNGE SPOTS

These are the places in the home where we watch TV, read a book, nap, meditate, or just hang out. They usually are, and should be, in the private parts of the home. Sometimes we prefer to be among other family members, either as a participant, or as a bystander to their activities. At other times we prefer to be alone in a remote quiet place. A secluded lounge chair on the edge of a room, a large overstuffed sofa, a chair and ottoman in the corner of an office may all offer places to relax and unwind at the end of a stressful day. Offer places for several to hang out and quiet places for just one.

CREATING HOUSES THAT WORK FOR LIFE

Entertainment Areas May Offer:
- Larger scale and smaller scale furniture with varied styles of seating
- View of TV from many vantage points
- Game table with appropriate lighting
- Space for a billiard/ping pong table
- Kitchenette or wet bar
- Natural light with light level control window treatments

Conversation Places Should Provide:
- Varied styles of seating
- Away from other activities
- Intimate scale for two or three people
- Surfaces for refreshments and accessories
- Lighting for different effects

Lounging Spots Should:
- Be in a quiet zone
- Provide natural light and views
- Have task lighting and ambient lighting
- Be on an intimate scale for one or two people

INSIDE OUT AND OUTSIDE IN

Taking the inside out and bringing the outside in, often creates our most cherished places. Courtyards, covered porches, secluded patios and sunrooms offer us privacy, shelter and a connection with the natural environment that most interior spaces just cannot provide. It is imperative in a house that works for life to incorporate places in and outside of the home that replenish the body, mind and spirit through the sound of water, texture of the earth and warmth of the sun.

CREATING HOUSES THAT WORK FOR LIFE

The light that makes these places so wonderful may also affect them negatively. Light control is a critical aspect for the proper performance of rooms, either indoor or outdoor. The angle in which sunlight enters is higher in the summer months than the winter. We can take advantage of this higher angle by including overhangs that shade the undesired heat of summer light, but permit the light to enter and warm the space in winter. Window treatments of many types are available for privacy but I recommend exterior mechanisms for light control.

This view is the western sky from my sunroom during sunset.

Sunrooms or areas surrounded by natural light and exterior views are in high demand with most consumers. The majority of additions built on existing houses include a sunroom or a space that brings the outside in. Natural light and how it enters the space determines the success of these places. The importance of southern exposure is obvious but a room that is glazed on three sides is preferred. Morning light filters in from the east, the warmth of the southern sun fills the room at midday and the restful light of the evening enters as the sun sets on the western horizon.

We added this space to function as my conference room. The intent was to provide an accessible space with natural light and views. The room became so much more. It is a wonderful place to be enjoyed in all seasons, to sit and watch a winter snowfall, to be warmed by the sunlight on a cool day, or cooled in the summer breeze.

CREATING HOUSES THAT WORK FOR LIFE

OVERHANG DIMENSION DETERMINED BY SUMMER SUN ANGLE
SUMMER SUN ANGLE
WINTER SUN ANGLE
40 DEGREES
WALL
WINDOW
80 DEGREES
DRAWING MUST BE TO SCALE
SOLAR SHADING - OVERHANG SIZING RULES FOR SOUTH FACING OVERHANGS

This helps determine the dimension of overhang required for shading. You might need to acquire more information to ensure this calculation. Not all latitudes will be represented with these angles.

All spaces should have operable, well-insulated windows, but it is extremely important for the sunroom. Cross ventilation will cool the space and assist in bringing the outdoors in. The views of the surrounding landscape also add to the experience. Windows may frame or accentuate a particularly pleasing view.

Natural light tends to take precedence in a sunroom space, but don't take the importance of electric light fixtures for granted. The right lighting extends the pleasures of this space into the evening hours. Soft ambient light may illuminate the evening in a manner just as enjoyable as the natural light of day.

The overhang on my sunroom is 36". I followed the diagram above to determine the depth.

This room is not just wonderful in the daytime hours, it is a great place to relax in the evening.

CREATING HOUSES THAT WORK FOR LIFE

View from sunroom onto the frozen fish pond and waterfall.

Garden areas that are easy to access and maintain allow all of us the opportunity to connect with the earth. Research indicates that this connection is extremely important to the human experience. The desire to connect with the earth intensifies as we age. Gardening is enjoyed by all generations, but most often enhances an elder person's life.

As we age and our bodies are no longer as agile as they once were. Stooping and bending over to garden may become quite difficult. Raised garden beds make the act of gardening easier and more convenient for all gardeners. They lessen the burden of bending and stooping, are accessible and provide containers for composted, nutrient rich soil. If space is limited, gardening in large pots placed on a small patio will still satisfy a gardener's desire to feel the earth within their hands and watch the flowers grow.

A challenging economic climate combined with the movement to be earth friendly, or "green", are generating more and more people's interest in the propagation and growth of their own food. Whether growing edibles or flowers, gardening will promote activity, enhance beauty and stimulate the soul.

Outdoor places expand the living areas of your home. You might want an area with a fire pit to roast marshmallows in the evenings or a dining table and chairs. Barbeque grills, bars and outdoor kitchens are available in most home improvement stores.

CREATING HOUSES THAT WORK FOR LIFE

A sloped backyard offers the perfect opportunity for a waterfall and fish pond.

A fishpond may be a main attraction, my grandchildren love to watch and feed the fish.

The outdoor place might be a small porch tucked in the corner of the most modest home or the grand courtyard of a country estate, but regardless of their size or grandeur, these places truly enhance the quality of dwelling.

STORAGE - CLOSETS, GARAGES, & BASEMENTS

A common complaint with most housing is not enough storage space. Storage comes in a multitude of areas. We typically think of closets, but shelving, cabinets, built-in window seats, and furniture also provide useful storage space.

Some things require concealed storage, but many of the things we have can be displayed. Open storage spaces add to the character and beauty of the home. Built-in shelves, display cabinets and niches offer an opportunity to personalize the space with your stuff. Showcasing items that have meaning allows us to surround ourselves with memories of family, friends, travel, and good times.

CLOSETS

Walk-in closets are very popular in new houses, many people request them even in the children's and spare bedrooms. Walk-in closets require circulation space within the closet.

113

CREATING HOUSES THAT WORK FOR LIFE

This clear floor space offers no additional storage but the shelves are easier to reach. The desire for walk-in closets is easily fulfilled when the budget for the project permits, but usually the budget is tight and the additional square footage required is the first to be eliminated.

Most older homes do not offer enough storage. When remodeling an existing home, creative ways to gain storage are needed. A typical closet is 2' deep. This is just enough space for a hanger to fall freely within the space. The doors are standard height of 6'8" inches with a header across the top. The clothes rod is placed 1' out from the back wall and a 12" deep shelf is placed above the rod. This shelf is very difficult to access due to the limited height of the door opening. When we extend the doors all the way to the ceiling, using an 8' high door and opening, the storage space becomes similar to a walk-in. The circulation remains in the living area, not the closet, and the shelves are much easier to access. If space permits, the closet can be made a little deeper to really open it up, and the floor space can be used for storage, not just circulation. The doors become a very important part of this solution. By-pass doors are ok, but only half of the closet is accessible at a time. By-fold doors tend to work well, but the width of each panel cannot exceed 18".

The weight of the door becomes a factor in how well it operates. Wider widths tend to come out of their tracts easily. Doors that swing out interfere with the circulation space and are difficult for wheelchair users to operate. Pocket doors work the best but require addition wall space for the doors to recede into, which usually does not exist.

This closet was built with 8' high bi-fold doors and is 30" deep providing an easier accessed upper shelf and additional storage on the floor.

GARAGES

A standard two car garage is 20' x 20' with a 16' wide door. This size might have been appropriate when cars were smaller and people didn't have so much stuff, but they do not work for today's families. Vehicles are now larger and the need for more storage space in the garage is larger too.

CREATING HOUSES THAT WORK FOR LIFE

We need more circulation space to get into and out of the car, truck or SUV. Cars seats, baby carriers, groceries, supplies and people usually come and go from this space. Most families have two cars and would prefer if they both could be stored in the garage. Elder users need to have easy accessibility for a wheelchair, cane, walker or personal assistance. Garages should be at least 24' x 24' to comfortably house two cars and meet the circulation and storage needs of most families.

BASEMENTS

Basements are often used as storage spaces but many are also used as additional living space. I find it interesting when clients request the entire basement be converted into a family entertainment area without considering where all of the stuff that currently fills the entire basement will go. They usually claim they will get rid of everything or find another place in the house for it. Realistically, this is never going to happen. It is important to maintain some storage in the basement for most families. Shelves help organize and make things easier to find. Cabinets can conceal items and provide more usable space.

Rooms built specifically for storage allow other spaces in the basement to be used more effectively. When storage space isn't provided we tend to let things pile up on the perimeter and they eventually take over the entire space. When rooms are designated as storage spaces our behavior improves and we usually keep our belongings confined within the designated areas.

Basements should be designed with the same flexibility as the main level of the house. Usage requirements may change over the years or even on a daily basis.

> *I designed a basement for a family that needed an additional family room, but also loved to conduct family ping-pong tournaments. There was not enough space for both so we solved the problem by placing the family area next to the storage area, separating them with a set of pocket doors. The furniture was movable and could easily be placed on the perimeter of the room and still be functional. The ping pong table was stored in the adjacent space. It conveniently rolled out and unfolded in the center of the family room. With little effort, this room served both functions effectively.*

CREATING HOUSES THAT WORK FOR LIFE

Basement areas should never be used as a bedroom without meeting proper ventilation and egress requirements. Basements that are not walk-outs or do not have egress windows typically have only one way out. If that staircase is blocked by fire there is no other alternative. Too often homeowners decide to take advantage of the addition space of a basement without understanding the consequences that may occur. We have building codes to ensure our health and safety. Bedroom spaces have more requirements than any other space in the home. They must have ventilation and egress; this means operable windows large enough to escape from in case of a fire. A typical basement window is not large enough and is placed too high in the wall to meet the egress regulation. Fresh air also factors in; a certain percentage of the square footage must be met in window openings. Egress from a basement is crucial if the basement is used for anything other than storage, but it is a code requirement for bedroom space.

As mentioned before, it can be a challenge to make basement spaces work for all users. Accessibility will always be an issue. Alternative options are available, lifts, elevators and accessible walk-out installations, but these options can be expensive.

Creative lighting techniques in a basement enhances a rather dark space.

Another kitchen in this basement for entertaining large groups really works for this family.

CREATING HOUSES THAT WORK FOR LIFE

EASY MAINTENANCE

When specifying materials for houses that work for life we need to consider ease of maintenance, durability and whether they are eco-friendly. It is common for these requirements to conflict with one another. Vinyl is easy to maintain and qualifies as average for durability, but is toxic to produce. Many of the products available to replace the use of vinyl are expensive in comparison. Wood and composites are eco-friendly materials but without the proper coatings to protect them from the elements, their durability is lessened. Painting your house every few years is not considered easy maintenance. Brick and stone are very durable and easily maintained, but how far they have traveled to reach the site determines how they rate on the "green" scale. It is not my intention to make all of this sound so difficult, but it is complex and important to gain an understanding of what materials are selected for the construction or renovation of your home. easily maintained but how far they have traveled to reach the site determines how they rate on the eco-friendly scale. It is not my intention to make all of this sound so difficult, but it is complex and important to gain an understanding of what materials are selected for the construction or renovation of your home.

The materials used on the exterior of houses can sometimes be dictated by the developer. Architectural committees prescribe requirements for the usage of a particular percentage of stone, brick or wood and may prohibit the use of vinyl or other materials. The style of the house, the pitch of the roof and square footage minimums are often regulated. Local covenants and restrictions should be investigated thoroughly and considered before the purchase of a site for a new house or of an existing home.

Current technology and the desire for energy efficient and eco-friendly materials have resulted in influx of new products in the market place. Conduct your research, evaluate your needs and select the materials accordingly.

> The materials used on the exterior of houses can sometimes be dictated by the developer and architectural committees.

CONCLUSION

8

Whether we live modestly or in luxury, in a mass produced or custom built home, we all deserve to live and dwell in homes that empower us and enhance life's experiences.

CONCLUSION

Our country is feeling extremely proud. We have just elected our first African-American president. Diversity and equality are virtues the world respects and admires. Inclusiveness of all races, socioeconomic classes, religions and abilities, is an aspiration of our society. However, our housing forces segregation of generations, socioeconomic levels and people with physical disabilities.

Demographics are researched and studied for our housing market. Subdivisions are specifically targeted to certain age groups and socioeconomic levels of home buyers, our elders retire to gated communities for only their generation to reside. Those with physical challenges are limited; not by their *abilities* but by the *inability* of houses to support their needs.

The dynamic of the family has been revered for ages. The success of the family is due, in part, to the age diversity of its members. Young inspire the old, elders teach the young. The interaction between generations enriches all of our lives, but our society is losing site of this valuable attribute. We separate our children from elders, beginning in daycare and throughout their education. Our elders are removed from society and placed in nursing, assisted living and retirement homes.

Our homes should support trans-generational interaction not prohibit it. They should be visit-able for people of all abilities. Whether we live modestly or in luxury, in a mass produced or custom built home, we all deserve to live and dwell in homes that empower us and enhance life's experiences.

Designing for a multitude of users and uses can be a daunting task, but for a house to work for life we must look at all possibilities. We must acknowledge the issues of typical housing, understand the need for personalized space, consider the attributes and deficiencies of the site, follow a public to private concept and allow function and aesthetics to have equal power in the design process. When we apply these design principles and rethink the "way things have always been done", we can achieve the goal of creating houses that are ecologically responsible and provide comfort, security and support for the tasks of day to day life for all generations.

CONCLUSION

I love old people, their wisdom and wit, their accomplishments and skills, their advice and life's stories. They have so much to offer and are seldom engaged in doing so. We all should have the privilege of living with an elder or having an older neighbor. Back porch visits on crisp fall days, or sharing plants and tips in the garden with elders, have been some of my life's most pleasant memories.

BIBLIOGRAPHY

Howe, Jeffery. The Houses We Live: An Identification Guide to the History and Style of American Domestic Architecture. London, UK: PRC Publishing, 2002

Jacobson, Max, Silverstein, Murray, Winslow, Barbara. Pattern of Home: The Ten Essentials of Enduring Design. Newtown, CT: Taunton Press, 2002

Marcus, Clare Cooper. House as a Mirror of Self: Exploring the Deeper Meaning of Home. Berkeley, Calif.: Conari Press, 1995

Moore, Charles. The Place of Houses. New York: Harper-Collins, 1992

Susanka, Sarah. The Not So Big House: A Blueprint for the Way We Really Live. Newtown, CT: Taunton Press, 1998

Winter, Steven, Associates. Passive Solar Design Construction Handbook. New York: John Wiley & Sons, 1998

Permaculture.org. Permaculture Research Institute. 03 Feb. 2009 <http//www.permaculture.org.au/about.php>.

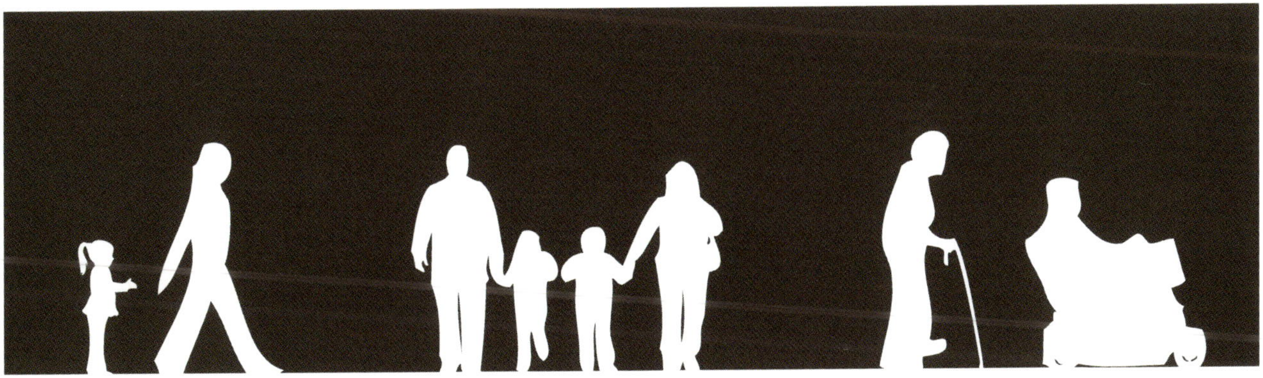